Reaction

Against the modern world

Peter King

SOCIETAS
essays in political
& cultural criticism

imprint-academic.com

Published in the UK by Societas
Imprint Academic, PO Box 200, Exeter EX5 5YX, UK

Published in the USA by Societas
Imprint Academic, Philosophy Documentation Center
PO Box 7147, Charlottesville, VA 22906-7147, USA

ISBN 9781845403478

A CIP catalogue record for this book is available from the
British Library and US Library of Congress

Contents

Acknowledgements	iv
Introduction	1
Only Correct	14
Reaction	31
Common Sense	62
Antimodern	95
Prejudice	132
Bibliography	153
Index	157

Acknowledgements

Writing is a solitary activity but also one that depends on the forbearance, co-operation and good will of others to provide the necessary quiet space. My wife, B, is the one who I have come to rely on most and I am grateful that her forbearance appears unlimited. My daughters, Helen and Rachel, are also a great support. One of the delights of being a parent is watching one's children grow up into young adults capable of forming their own arguments and challenging the received view that 'dad knows best'. This is certainly now the case with Helen and Rachel, who have graduated from passive supporters to genuine critics and whose views I now actively seek on the grounds that they are both much cleverer than me. They have been kind enough to listen to my ravings and on many occasions they have forced me to clarify my views and to improve my arguments.

While working on this book over the last couple of years I have gained much from debates and discussion with my students. All my students are part-time, attending at most one day per week at the university, spending the rest of the time working and living in the real world. They bring with them that all-important element that academic debate so often lacks – common sense – and I am grateful to them for putting an end to many of my flights of fancy.

My colleagues at De Montfort are as supportive a group of people as one could wish for, providing the ideal environment to spark new ideas and offering the time and space to develop them. I am particularly grateful to them because I know they disagree with much of what I have to say.

Finally, thanks are also due to Keith Sutherland and his colleagues for taking on this book. Their courage is matched only by their wisdom.

Peter King, November 2011

Introduction

I

Despite my best efforts I have struggled to come across anyone who actually refers to themselves as a reactionary. It is much more common to be labelled a reactionary by others: those so labelled might well include the Pope and many in the hierarchy of the Catholic Church; the Prince of Wales; those who write for journals like *The Salisbury Review* and *The Quarterly Review* (alongside their readers); as well as large parts of the Conservative party. Indeed the label tends to be used rather frequently, but only when it is applied to others. In recent times I have come across the label being attached to trade unionists in both the US and Britain who have taken a stand against government spending reductions and job cuts; English students protesting against increases in university tuition fees; street protestors in France arguing against changes to the retirement age; as well as senior Islamic clerics in Iran and ostensibly socialist dictators in North Africa. It seems that 'reaction' can be used to demonise anyone regardless of their beliefs or whether they might have anything in common with anyone else so labelled.

This recent usage is interesting because it has been more common for reactionaries to be taken as figures of fun. They are people who ignore the direction of history and insist on holding on to a bygone age. They refuse to accept things as they are. If we look at a thesaurus for synonyms of reactionary, we find words such as blimpish and obscurantist. Reaction is seen almost entirely as negative. It perhaps conjures up images of old men in tweeds fulminating against the world. For those brought up on popular culture they might be reminded of the ridiculous racist bigot Alf Garnett, or much more recently Al Murray's creation of the 'Pub Landlord', who refuses to countenance the possibility of women drinking pints. Reactionaries are bores and bigots and there is the tendency to assume that all they do is to indulge in splenetic, spittle-flecked diatribes against the world as it is, their fists bunched and blood pressure rising as they stand by ineffectively watching as the modern world carries on regardless. See, for example, the caricature of Steve Moxon's 'reactionary' book on immigration in the impeccably liberal journal *Progress*:

> The best thing about this book is that it saves you the cost of an evening in the pub. Just reading Moxon conjured up the filthy red carpet, the sticky counter, the smoky air and the swivel-eyed patron on the next stool, sharing his opinions.

There may be something in these images: there is undoubtedly some who act just like this over their gin at the 19th hole, or in their local after a pint or two. However, these are caricatures and this is not how the word is more frequently used now. Instead it applies to anyone who is opposed to change and progress. Importantly it need not matter what the changes proposed are. They might involve cuts in public services leading to job losses. But to oppose these is to be accused of reaction.

But it is not the case that trade unionists or Iranian clerics are becoming more intransigent but rather it seems that everyone now wants to be considered a progressive. So when the UK Coalition Government announced its long-term spending plans in October 2010, which consisted of £80 billion in cuts, the key argument that they wished to put across to the public was not that the spending plans were sensible or even workable, but that they were progressive. Indeed nearly a third of the accompanying document was taken up with an impact assessment crammed with statistics purporting to show that the wealthy would pay disproportionately more than the poor. Needless to say, the Labour opposition put much of their effort into trying to prove that the opposite was the case. The belief was that if the plans were shown not to be progressive they would somehow be seriously impaired, if not totally invalidated.

Progress is the word that everyone seems to want to own, and accordingly the insult *de jour* is reactionary. This instantly damns one's opponent: they are accused of rejecting progress; they do not grasp the future, but instead seek to hold onto the failures of the past. Instead of wanting the bright shiny optimism of the future they cling to the soiled past. How could anyone be so blinkered as to oppose change?

But the generalisation of progress means that anyone can be a reactionary, including trade unionists who oppose their members losing their jobs and Christians not prepared to accept changing attitudes to marriage and sexuality. Both these groups might argue that they have merely stood still and would like to continue doing what they have always done. But the situation is even more complicated than this. There are those who have stood up for what they see as enduring Western liberal values, in the face of what they see as reactionary threats, who find themselves condemned as reactionaries: one can be a reactionary because one opposes reactionary ideas, or rather, one does so in the 'wrong' way.

This is evident in the response to what might be termed (with a due nod to the irony of the term) 'liberal reaction'. This is the view that Western societies, with their liberal democratic traditions based on human rights and tolerance, should not accept those elements within their society that would seek to overturn these traditions. The most significant examples of liberal reaction are the Dutch politicians Pim Fortuyn and Geert Wilders, who have argued against Muslim immigration on the grounds of Islam's supposed intolerance to Europe's post-Enlightenment values. These politicians have argued that the Dutch should not accept migrants who reject sexual and gender equality. Yet, so-called progressives on the left have taken the view that Fortuyn, who was an openly gay former sociology professor, was a fascist, and that Wilders was a right-wing extremist who was accordingly banned from entering the UK in 2009 on the grounds that he was a 'threat to one of the fundamental interests of society', namely 'community harmony', and that his presence might post a threat to public safety.[1] Both these politicians have been seen as reactionary because of the manner in which they have sought to protect western liberal values by opposing multiculturalism. Indeed Fortuyn was assassinated in 2002 as a result of his public statements. Wilders, who has to have 24-hour security because of threats

---

1 http://www.geertwilders.nl/images/images/letter-denying-geert-wilders-entry-into-uk.pdf accessed on 18 December 2010.

against him, was described in a BBC documentary in 2011 as the 'most dangerous man in Europe'.

What this suggests is that there is no stereotypical reactionary. Some might indeed prefer tweeds, as well as the odd glass of something, and others might be angry at the world and fulminate against it. However, others might take a much more considered view, and see it as entirely rational for them to argue as they do based on their own view of the world. Moreover, the manner in which they proceed may well be civilised, informed, and even ironic. Indeed some of the most effective forms of reaction are those using satire and ridicule, as in the work of the writer and journalist Auberon Waugh.[2]

So it would be a mistake to assume that there is only one form of reaction. There need be no commonality between reactionaries, and different commentators and thinkers will emphasise certain issues rather than others. There may be considerable disagreement between people who appear to be reactionary, and there may be little obviously in common with intellectual and populist reaction. As an example, we might suggest that fundamentalist Islam is reactionary, in terms of its attitudes towards modernity, but this does not mean that it is supported by British and European reactionaries who wish to protect what they see as a threatened Christian tradition, and nor is fundamentalism likely to be highly regarded down the pub. Moreover, none of these groups might actually choose to use the label 'reactionary' to refer to themselves.

But if this is so, just what does reaction consist of, and is there anything that ties these different views together? In this essay I wish to explore what, if anything, it is that reactionaries believe. We might suggest that they simply oppose, and this would be true: reactionaries, almost always, are against things. But this will not do as a definition. Many individuals and groups are against things — nuclear power, the death penalty, eating meat, global warming — and are as a result taken to be progressives. So we cannot just assume that simply one who opposes is a reactionary. We need to look elsewhere.

---

2 See Waugh (2001) for a sample of both his wit and reactionary attitudes.

But in doing so we are faced with an immediate problem. One cannot, properly speaking, be a reactionary *on principle*, in the way one can be a liberal or a socialist. There is no set of readily identifiable principles marked 'reactionary'. Reaction is not an ideology or set of beliefs (and it is this quality that allows the label to be used against so diverse a range of people and ideas). This does not mean, however, that reaction is unprincipled, opportunist or an unthinking response. We most certainly can say that it is possible to be a principled reactionary, in that we react *because* of the principles we have. Clearly if these particular principles were dominant then we would not be a reactionary, in that we would be in agreement with, rather than seeking to oppose, the status quo. One is a reactionary, therefore, because one is in a minority. But one is also reactionary by experience and through circumstance: we are turned into it because of what faces us, not because we are a priori reactionary. Of course, we might point to people who we know to have reacted in the past and who might well, conditions willing, do so again. But even here, this is because of a reason, not because they are reactionary *per se*.

Yet not everyone acts in this way and so cannot be covered by the label. People respond to stimuli in different ways: some might fulminate against change, while others are readily persuaded and take up the new ways with enthusiasm. So clearly we need some reason to understand why some people do react in a particular manner. We need to understand why some people agree with a particular state of affairs and others do not.

The first thing to appreciate is that there is a difference between the simple act of reacting, and reaction in the political or cultural sense as we mean it in this essay. We all, to one extent or another, react when we are confronted with a situation or when we feel we have been insulted or threatened. This is a natural response where our instincts kick in as a result of a particular stimulus. However, we intend here something more specific: the sense of being against a particular political and cultural situation. An example of this type of reaction is provided by Joseph de Maistre (1850, 1974), who was a leading contemporary opponent of the French Revolution and the Enlightenment thought that underpinned it. De Maistre was apparently a typical well-educated Savoyard lawyer until the effects of the French Revolution became apparent to him (Lebrun, 1988). Yet the Revolution turned him into an articulate and consistent reactionary opponent, who spent much of his considerable intellectual energy on denouncing the effect of the inheritance of the French Enlightenment. De Maistre was a reactionary both by circumstance and by temperament.

We might become a reactionary because we feel threatened, or because of what we have lost or fear we might lose. We feel the need to protect something, to preserve it, or perhaps even to regain it. De Maistre was famous for both his critique of revolution and for his call for a return to Throne and Altar, of what had gone wrong and what ought to be restored. But this is not enough: de Maistre would undoubtedly have gained more by complying with the French occupiers (Lebrun, 1988). But there was something about de Maistre that did not allow him to sit back and watch his country being occupied and be transformed according to Enlightenment ideals. He felt that he had to resist this physical and cultural invasion. It is this 'something' that has made him one of history's great reactionaries.

We may believe in something, but to say that we react is invariably to act negatively. We do not, as a rule, talk about reactionaries as being in support of positive change: we will rather refer to these sorts of people as progressives. So we need to be aware (as if we could not be) that reaction is always taken as a negative. It is always against something. This perhaps explains why reactionaries are in the minority: it is much more appealing to appear positive about the world than to oppose it. But it also informs us why there will always be reaction: the world is never as we would like it to be and things always go wrong.

As the (impeccably liberal) philosopher Karl Popper has argued, there are always unintended consequences. He points out that:

> it is one of the striking things about social life that *nothing ever comes off exactly as intended*. Things always turn out a little bit differently. We hardly ever produce in social life precisely the effect that we wish to produce, and we usually get things that we do not want into the bargain. Of course we act with certain aims in mind; but apart from these aims (which we may or may not really achieve) there are always certain unwanted conse-

> quences of our actions; and usually these unwanted consequences cannot be eliminated. To explain why they cannot be eliminated is the major task of social theory. (1989, p. 124, author's emphasis)

If we know 'that nothing comes off exactly as intended' then we are merely being rational in resisting the radical or adventurous change. This is indeed the starting point for the reactionary: things always do go wrong. And so their perspective will most definitely appear to be negative. This is precisely what is intended by reaction. But what is it that is wrong? We have suggested that reactionaries are those who oppose things; yet they do not necessarily all agree on what is wrong and so presumably on what the solutions might be. So, while we will need to generalise somewhat, we must do so without an excessive presumption of what is being opposed.

What I would suggest is the problem for reactionaries, whether it be de Maistre two centuries ago or contemporary thinkers, is the idea of the modern. Obviously this is a term that will need to be defined, but I shall be using the word to denote that which is the opposite of tradition. Reactionaries, quite simply, are anti-modernists and defenders of tradition. This being so, we can point to a number of elements of the modern world that reactionaries will tend to oppose, and these, in whole or in part, will apply whether we are talking about the Counter-Enlightenment or those who are writing today. These ideas are not tied to any particular political ideology or show any party preference. Indeed it is precisely because all the mainstream parties – be they left, right or centre – share many of the elements of modernity, that the reactionary view is itself so pertinent. It will also allow us to show that reaction operates on different levels. It can be intellectual and elitist, offering reasons for the preservation of a culture and against its repudiation by modernists and postmodernists. But it can also operate at the commonsense level, where there is a low level disquiet about the world and whether 'we' – it is always personalised – are being listened to by those who purport to represent us. There are those reactionaries who write books or comment in newspapers, and then those – a far greater number – who find themselves at odds with, or who have some disquiet about, the modern world. These types of reaction are quite distinct:

one is elitist and the other not, one supports the idea of high culture and the other tends only towards the popular, one is aware of politics and may engage with it while the other sees it as something others do. But both these views have things in common and it is the purpose of this essay to identify them and to elaborate on their significance.

So I wish to reclaim the idea of reaction and show that it is not merely a knee jerk response to the new or an attempt to protect certain vested interests. The view I wish to develop in this book is that there is some merit in reaction, even if it does remain negative and will doubtless always be unpopular and unfashionable. This is because so much of what is termed change and progress is ill thought out and bound to fail. Experience teaches of the inevitability of unintended consequences and so we should not be surprised that many, if not most, proposals for change will fail to achieve their ends and lead to problems that were not intended or foreseen. What makes reaction both necessary and ever present is the sheer inevitability of the failure of progress. And so as long as there is the call for progress, which is then acted upon, there will be the need for reaction. This might not stop all the mistakes being made, but it might act as a brake and slow down the speed of change. It might give us more of a chance to hold onto what we know works and not lose all that is valuable in our headlong dash for progress.

II

However, there is an immediate problem that needs to be attended to before we can proceed any further. We have stated that reaction is a concern with the consequences of change. But how does this differ from conservatism? Are we merely conflating reaction with conservatism, and if so, why is it really necessary to discuss reaction as if it were a distinct entity? Indeed, a standard dictionary definition of a reactionary will usually include the term 'extreme conservative'. Reactionaries are seen as being at the extreme end of the spectrum of conservative politics. Reaction is therefore just a particularly vociferous and possibly violent form of conservatism.

It may well be the case that many, indeed most, reactionaries see themselves as conservative, although some might choose other terms such as nationalist, primitivist or traditionalist. This problem is only compounded by the fact that, as we have seen, in most cases the term 'reactionary' is used as a form of abuse and is not adopted as a positive designation. Those individuals who are properly reactionary might not choose to so label themselves so or might prefer to choose something very different.

What we need to do, therefore, is to separate out reaction from conservatism and to show that there is indeed some space between them. This will not be a completely open space: there are bridges between the two and at some places perhaps even a merging. It is sometimes difficult to point to an exact place where conservatism stops and reaction starts. However, a useful starting point in creating this distinction, particularly in the light of the need to remain aware of the lack of a hard distinction, is the discussion of the conservative disposition by Michael Oakeshott in his essay 'On being conservative' (1991). This is a subtle discussion of what it is to be conservative and so allows us to distinguish between it and the reactionary impulse.

Oakeshott describes conservatism as a disposition rather than a doctrine: 'it is to be disposed to think and behave in certain manners ... it is to be disposed to make certain kinds of choices' (p. 407). Conservatives prefer what is current or present rather than to look elsewhere and they do so because it is familiar. Oakeshott particularly stresses this notion of familiarity. We relate to what we know and what is close to us, and the more we are able to enjoy this the better. He suggests, however, that this is tempered by a sense of loss. The conservative disposition is strongest where there is much to enjoy and therefore a sense that there might be much to lose. According to Oakeshott:

> To be conservative, then, is to prefer the familiar to the unknown, to prefer the tried to the untried, fact to mystery, the actual to the possible, the limited to the unbound, the near to the distant, the sufficient to the superabundant, the convenient to the perfect, present laughter to utopian bliss. Familiar relationships and loyalties will be preferred to the allure of the more profitable attachments; to acquire and to enlarge will be less important than to keep, to cultivate and to enjoy; the grief

> of loss will be more acute than the excitement of novelty and promise. (pp. 408-9)

Conservatives resist change not because what is new is worse than what went before, but because what has been lost was familiar and known: it is something to which they have become attached. The conservative finds no favour in innovation, seeing only uncertainty and loss. So, for Oakeshott, the disposition to be conservative is 'warm and positive in respect to enjoyment, and correspondingly cool and critical in respect to change and innovation'. (p. 412)

Conservatives, according to Oakeshott, do not wish to have views imposed on them by others, nor do they wish to impose their worldview on anyone else. We can tolerate views that we may not agree with, but we have no wish to be ruled by them. The role of government therefore is to prevent this by providing a form of order so that conflicts between different beliefs and activities can be resolved.[3] It should do this not by imposing uniformity or conformity but 'by enforcing general rules of procedure upon all subjects alike' (p. 428). Oakeshott suggests that the role of government is to pacify and to instil a sense of moderation. It should seek:

> to restrain, to deflate, to pacify and to reconcile; not to stoke the fires of desire, but to damp them down. And all this, not because passion is vice and moderation virtue, but because moderation is indispensable if passionate men are to escape being in an encounter of mutual frustration. (p. 432)

Oakeshott paints a picture of the conservative as being comfortable and seeking security to enjoy what is familiar: it is where stability reigns and so we are able to enjoy our chosen activities free from the imposition of others and from government. This is in many ways an appealing vision, but it is a thoroughly complacent one. What, however, are we to make of the situation, like that of Joseph de Maistre, where much of what he took to be familiar had been lost? What do we do when the vision of another is imposed upon us and we have no form of remedy? We may indeed seek to preserve the familiar, but what happens if it is no longer pos-

---

[3] Note that just as there is a continuum between reaction and conservatism there is a similar overlap with classical liberalism.

sible to preserve, and that much of what we treasure has already been lost? What do we do then, when, as Oakeshott suggests, the conservative disposition is itself weak? Is this not where reaction comes in?

As we have suggested reaction is often the result of the threat or actuality of loss. It is where we have lost what we treasure or we have clear grounds to fear its loss. We can suggest, then, that reaction is where we are incapable of complacency. We are not capable of simply enjoying those familiar activities but must fight for them. It is where we are so threatened that we cannot merely continue as before. As we shall see, reactionaries may act in a number of ways – from direct action to withdrawal – but what they are not able to do is simply act without regard for the consequences of their actions. Oakeshott does not deal with what happens when the conservative disposition is weak or absent, but we can suggest that the conservative has but two options: to withdraw or to fight.

So reaction can be differentiated from conservatism. But, we should not expect the division to be hard and fast. There may well be a point where reaction and conservatism meet, and where complacency turns into diffidence, anger and perhaps even resistance. It is here that reaction effectively takes over from conservatism.

III

But the fact that there remains a connection might lead some – particularly those with a predisposition against conservatism – to presume that there is in fact a continuum or even no substantive difference between reaction and conservatism. For example, Corey Robin (2011) appears to see little distinction between them. For him, it is all a matter of tactics: if conservatives cannot preserve the familiar (or in his terms, maintain their particular unity of interests) then they will readily turn to violence and force. In the face of persistent calls for equality and social justice conservatives will act to defend their interests and will do so with violence. Robin's argument is a highly contentious one and is dependent on a particular conception of conservatism as illegitimate precisely because he sees it as inimical to his conception of the social good. We might say therefore that it suits his purpose to label all conservatives as reactionaries.

Such self-serving arguments are not uncommon with regard to reaction. It is an unsought-for label, used as a torment rather than a badge of honour. My aim in this essay is to assess whether this is entirely fair, by seeking a fuller understanding of what reaction is really about. It considers whether it can ever be a respectable position to hold, or is the term always destined to be little more than a low-level insult, a means of ending a debate by stating that your opponent is not being serious? It details where reaction has come from and why it still persists and why it remains necessary. I shall, therefore, take the notion of reaction seriously and see where it leads.

My argument proceeds in the following manner. Chapter one sets up some of the key arguments with regard to reaction by juxtaposing it with the idea of change. Change is seen as a problem where it is becomes an end itself, where it is reduced to a slogan without any substance. Following Burke, I argue that change is acceptable where it seeks to correct a situation rather than to create something new or original. The chapter will also open up a key distinction between elitist and commonsense notions of reaction. This will be further developed in the next two chapters.

Chapter two considers the idea of reaction is some detail. It begins by considering the development of the term and its linkage with progress and revolution. The idea of reaction is defined using the work primarily of Edmund Burke (1992, 1999a, 1999b, 1999c, 1999d) and Joseph de Maistre (1850, 1974, 1993, 1996, 1998). A key issue is to consider how far reactionaries can be active in politics and whether one should rather expect a more fatalistic position of withdrawal. The role of the reactionary as a critic of the modern and a defender of high culture will be explored.

But there is a further form of reaction, one based on common sense, and this is considered in chapter three. This will be seen as an inchoate and inarticulate form of reaction based on a bewilderment of the world as it is and a belief that the majority – 'we' – are not been listened to by the governing establishment. This form of reaction, however, is seldom in any way active, but examples of it manifesting into something more concrete and formal are discussed, particularly the US Tea Party movement.

These two forms of reaction are distinct, but they are connected by one thing, namely, their distrust of the modern. This is considered in chapter four, which defines the idea of the antimodern and the importance of tradition. Modernism is defined and criticised and is followed by a discussion of the postmodern and what is wrong with it. A number of views on the antimodern are explored including the Prince of Wales's notion of harmony with the natural world and René Guénon's perennialist philosophy. These are linked to reaction as important critiques of modernity.

In the final chapter there is some attempt to determine the full importance of reaction. Reaction will be seen to rely on the idea of prejudice, but this, following Burke, will be shown to be a natural cognitive style for most of us, and a corrective to the rationalism of progress. The problem of rehabilitating concepts such as reaction and prejudice will be at the centre of this discussion. In particular, I shall consider whether the label of reactionary matters: is there any utility in using the term and why should we persist with it. The answer, for those that get that far, will come as no surprise.

This book is therefore an attempt to consider an unpopular and misunderstood word. Whether it is justified and the term can ever be rehabilitated, and whether it ever should be, are questions to be settled by the arguments that follow. The aim, however, is not to be gratuitously contrary or to present an argument merely because it is unpopular. There is, I hope, no affectation here or attempt to jump on a bandwagon (even if there were one). But by the same token I do not consider this to be a polemic. Yes, it is committed and sympathetic to the idea of reaction and antimodernism, but not at the expense of all things. I do not consider reaction to be an extreme position: I see it as an unpopular term to describe a fairly common set of beliefs, and that is why I consider this book to both necessary and timely. Overwhelming popular opposition to, for example, high levels of immigration and the European single currency has become harder to disparage as bigoted xenophobia, so perhaps the progressive tide is beginning to turn.

Chapter One

Only Correct

I

2010 was the year when change became a problem. It was the year in which the electorate in Britain could not come to a firm conclusion about what sort of government it would like to have, and so ended up with one it could not have predicted. It might then be portrayed as a year of indecision. But by the end of the year the nation's capital was defaced by a series of violent protests against some of the first acts of this unexpected government. 2010 was also the year where much change was promised, big debates were had about public spending, taxation and the future of the economy, but not much actually happened, indeed public spending was higher at the end of 2010 than at the start. So it was a year in which change was talked about a lot – and there was indeed a change of government – but not much was actually different at the end of the year from the start. But despite this there were some people vexed enough to protest, break windows and drop fire extinguishers on policemen.

Now it is entirely proper to say that many of the promised changes were merely being stored up for 2011 and beyond, and there is a lot of truth in this. But the happenings, and non-happenings, of 2010 are instructive nevertheless. What it showed was a combination of two apparently contradictory things: change and sameness. In many ways it was a pivotal year, with a change of government, and the formation of a coalition at that; the acceptance of the need to cut back on public expenditure and deal with public and private debt; and the beginning of resistance to these cutbacks. Yet, much of the daily life of the average Briton remained unchanged: life just went on as it ever did. We had a new government with an apparently new attitude towards the economy and politics, but they seemed to look much like the last lot, using the same words, acting in the same ways, and we seemed to have just as much scepticism towards them. So what really had changed?

2010 was also the year that the great audacious hope of US politics, the one who was to bring change, hit the reality of electoral politics. Barack Obama took up the presidency in January 2009 buoyed by a wave of enthusiasm and general warmth: here was a man who really would 'be the change'. Yet less than two years later he saw the Democrat's majority in the Senate drastically reduced and their control of the House of Representatives replaced with one of the biggest Republican majorities in a century. More generally, Obama's policies had been criticised by the emerging Tea Party movement, which was worried that the President was seeking to turn America into a European-style social democracy. But on the other hand, Obama was criticised from the left for not moving fast enough on issues like climate change, ending the war in Afghanistan and closing the Guantanamo Bay detention camp. Apparently, Obama was offering too much change for some and not enough for others and so was getting attacked from both sides. Perhaps he was just another politician after all, one who made promises he could not keep and who said things he did not really mean.

So in both countries there were people claiming that there was too much change and too little change: it was too quick or too slow. I have no real desire here to discuss what did, or might, change as a result of the election of the Conservative-Liberal Democratic coalition government in the UK. Nor do I wish to explore whether President Obama is a closet socialist or a weak liberal. I am all too aware that the political situation in either country might develop considerably and in a way that cannot be predicted. My purpose is rather to consider the notion of change itself. What united politics in the UK and the USA in 2010 – and perhaps in every year before and those since – was the propensity to proclaim the virtues of change.

It seems that all politicians want to do is to change things. It is a rare politician who delights in stability, and seeks to do very little. Not many politicians would choose to follow Ronald Reagan who apparently expressed the wish that his officials, 'Don't just do something, stand there!', and who purportedly said that while hard work never killled anyone, he wasn't inclined to take that sort of a risk. Instead of Reagan's easy complacency – which I mean as a compliment – we have politicians seeking to do as much as they can as quickly as they can, all the while being judged by those who complain, not that things are changing, but that it is too slow or the wrong sort of change.

The question therefore is why do politicians want to change things with such ardour? Why do they feel they have to? Of course, it might be because the situation that they inherit necessitates swift action and far-reaching reform. But all too often what politicians argue for is the idea of change itself: they don't seem just to have a particular goal in mind, but instead see creating change as an end in itself. We can speculate that it is because this is what they actually see politicians are for: that they are 'change agents' or some other such unpleasant term.

But politicians are not the only ones to blame. They only do things because the electorate – those who must suffer the changes – empower them. So why does the electorate let them? Why does the electorate consistently vote for people on the back of claims to create change? Are things really that bad? Or do they just get bored easily?

One answer may be the manner in which we perceive change as a general concept. Change, because it is still yet to happen, can always be portrayed as positive, and as better than what we currently have or had before. Because the change has not yet occurred it cannot be gainsaid (except, of course, by an even grander promise of change). To promote change is to promise that things will be better and there is not yet any evidence to say that it won't.

But, we might point to many past changes, to those occasions when the promise of change has proved to be an illusion. After all, it is not hard to make the point that the next change appears necessary only because of the failure of the last one. We can look at the effect that our societies have had on the natural environment: how our technologies, our ever-growing populations, and our exploitation of natural resources have created changes that we would not have deliberately sought, whether it be pollution, poverty or desertification. We can point to the fact that many of these supposed crises and problems come about as a result of past action. Climate change, we are told, is due to human action not inaction; the financial crisis of 2008 was due to people taking too many risks and not playing safe. It seems that quite a few problems have been due to action rather than inaction. There is an unpredictability about change: despite our optimism we may not really know what it is that we are doing.

What this leads to is a sense of things being out of control. There are too many big issues that are beyond us, whether it be climate change or the credit crunch. Many issues are connected in ways we struggle to comprehend and that we can only come to terms with using hindsight. At the time, however, these problems sneak up on us with no real warning. We get caught by surprise, and we quickly shift from being calm and confident to being in a panic. Indeed the effects are very serious, whether it be the effects of unemployment, repossession, inflation or worry over the cost of our children's university education.

There is now just too much uncertainty and we lack the capability to follow what is happening. There appears to us to be no pattern in what is happening: things are certainly changing, but we have lost track of how and why.

But if this is so, then why do politicians and their supporters still seek more change? Why do they feel that things can get better, despite the evidence? Indeed how can they claim that unless things change, that unless governments spend more, intervene more, reform institutions, we risk catastrophe? Why does the dull repetition of failure not curtail the call for change?

Yet there is no end to the call for change. The way to deal with climate change is not inaction, but to act differently. As we shall see, there are even those who call for a 'sustainability revolution' (Prince of Wales, 2010, p. 3): we need a revolution — a rapid and perhaps violent change — in order to ensure we can endure. Bad change does not lead to the call for an end to progress, merely the contention that it was the wrong sort of change.

So the problem is that change becomes an end it itself: it becomes the mantra of politics, indeed its very purpose. Idealistic young people go into politics to change things, to make the world a better place. If one wishes to make one's name one does not stand still but instead moves very fast and seeks to achieve as much as one can as quickly as possible. Modern politics is about movement, and never the status quo.

What I wish to suggest is that we have our view of change quite wrong. Instead of seeing it as a good thing, we ought to see change as the problem. We ought to seek less of it rather than more, and that the aim of politics should be to seek a period of stability and stasis. We should seek what we might actually call a period of correction.

One of Edmund Burke's most famous sayings is that 'A state without the means of some change is without the means of its conservation' (Burke, 1999b, p, 108). This is sometimes used to suggest that conservatives should not oppose change, but rather engage with it, and that without change there is no possibility of survival. The result is that Burke can be, and *is*, used to justify political change, and to make it respectable for conservatives.

But what is less frequently quoted is what Burke says immediately after this sentence:

> Without such means it might even risqué the loss of that part of the constitution which it wished the most religiously to preserve. The two principles of conservation and correction operated strongly at the two critical periods of the restoration and Revolution, when England found itself without a king. At both those periods the nation had lost the bond of union in their antient edifice; they did not, however, dissolve the whole fabric. On the contrary, in both cases they regenerated the deficient part of the old constitution through the parts which were not impaired. They kept the old parts exactly as they were, that the part recovered might be suited to them. (Burke, 1999b, pp., 108-9)

Burke is writing in response to a request for his views on the French Revolution and whether he would agree with those in England who argued that the French were merely doing what the English had done in their Glorious Revolution of 1688, namely overthrow an illegitimate monarch. Burke, however, argues that the revolution of 1688 did not involve the overthrow of a monarch so much as a situation where the English used their traditional and considered Constitution to correct a deficiency that had arisen through the *abdication* of an unsuitable monarch. The Constitution was not set aside, but rather was used and followed in order to repair the deficiency and so continue on much as it always had done. The decisions taken in 1688 were not, according to Burke, acts of repudiation but rather acts of repair. The deficiency caused by the abdication of an unsuitable king was remedied using those parts of the Constitution that still held fast. The result was that the traditions of the country were strengthened rather than weakened.[4]

Burke was here seeking to deflect the accusation that the French, with their capture and imprisonment of their monarch and usurpation of his authority, were in some manner mimicking the English. The French, however, had committed the treachery of innovation and operated according to the fiction that a monarch could be replaced if he no longer governed according to the will of the people. Burke showed that this was opposed to those actions of the English, who had merely sought to protect their constitution and ensure a recovery and not a revolution. We should note here that Burke talks only of conservation and correction and makes no mention of reform or improvement. Change is necessary not to modernise but to maintain and preserve what is ancient. Change is not something to relish but rather it is something to be got over; it is something to endure or suffer as best we can. And the best means to get through it is by using our working traditions to salve those parts that need repair.

So, to follow Burke, we only change because it is necessary to do so, and we use what still works to remake what is deficient. We do not innovate or invent, and we do not rush our change. What we have to do is to slow down, to ensure that we retain control. We change only to preserve.

Burke's argument here is commonly seen as a conservative position. But I would suggest it is more than this: it is a *reactionary* stance. This is the term that I wish to explore in some detail. I want to consider what it means to be a reactionary, where we wish to keep 'the old parts exactly as they were, that the part recovered might be suited to them' (Burke, 1999b, p, 109).

---

[4] Some might see in Burke's argument a rather romantic Whiggishness. This, however, is beside the point: what matters is the justification for change.

II

Reaction is most often portrayed as either extreme or as obscure. It can be described as angry, fulminating, counter-revolutionary, as an attempt to undo the modern world. It can be militant and possibly even violent as was the case with Italian extremists in the 1970s following the ideas of Julius Evola (Sedgwick, 2004). Evola saw the modern world as effeminate and wished it destroyed and replaced with what he saw as the true masculine tradition (Evola, 2002, 2003). Some of his followers took his work rather too literally, using bombs and assassination as a means to further this aim. But reaction can also be portrayed as blimpish, as out of touch with the real world, seeking instead a return to some ideal (that probably never really existed) when children did as they were told and were not heard to comment on it, when women were merely decorous, and the map was a reassuring pink colour. Reactionaries can therefore be seen as angry, perhaps even demented extremists railing against the modern world, or else as fantasists looking for a return to some mythical golden age while expressing bewilderment at the current state of the world.

In both cases reaction can be painted as active. It is political action, and just another means to create change. It is an engagement with modernity and an attempt to correct it, invert it or destroy it. Reactionaries are battling against progress. According to this view, reactionaries do things and they do so in a very noticeable manner, even if all they achieve is very little other than pointing to the ridiculous nature of their views. Reaction is therefore merely a particular form of political engagement, albeit a minority one and perhaps one necessarily doomed to failure: the clock cannot be turned back and the world cannot be unmade. We cannot readily unlearn what is common knowledge and return to an earlier and purer state of naiveté where we merely accepted things and did not seek to question them.

But if we acknowledge the very real possibility, indeed probability, of failure to achieve our aims, we are then led to a different view: that we should not be actively engaged with politics and reform. If we cannot possibly succeed then we should not seek to create change at all. This is precisely because democracy cannot be turned back: once we have allowed mass participation and the equal representation of all we cannot turn it back. We have no proper mechanism to do so that is not overly destructive of the very things that we wish to preserve. Nor should a reactionary fall into the trap of attempting to use the same methods as the revolutionary and the modernist: to do this is to play by another's game. The role of the reactionary therefore, as Nicolas Gomez Davila[5] has suggested, is to create suspicion about modernity. The reactionary should seek to sow seeds of doubt within their contemporaries. They should question the idea of progress and the hubris that underpins it. They should challenge the idea central to modernity that things are improving and that this is because humanity has learned to control its own destiny. They can point to examples in history such as the Holocaust and the Rwandan genocide, when this hubris has led to mass murder, and they can show how the two great movements for radical progress in the 20th century – communism and fascism – led to terror and created untold human misery.

Adopting this view of reaction is to place oneself on the outside. It is to resign as a player in the game and instead sit on the sidelines and merely comment. We know the consequences of political action and so seek to create suspicion and doubt.

Suspicion is where we have some reason not to take what we see or have been told at face value. We suspect something is not as it seems. We doubt what we are told to believe. To be suspicious is to show scepticism towards authority and received wisdom. Reactionaries believe that there are grounds for their doubt. There is some reason to believe that something is wrong and that we should mistrust those in authority. The reactionary wants us to appreciate that political action is never straightforward. Progress cannot be assured and so we cannot always believe what is being said to us. We should be suspicious of the grand plan and the easy optimism of the progressive and the utopian.

The suspicion, however, need not be based on anything specific. Rather we might have a more general belief that all

---

[5] None of Davila's works have been translated into English. A sample of his work, which mainly takes the form of aphorisms, can be found at http://don-colacho.blogspot.com (accessed 6 February 2011).

is not as it appears. The suspicion may still be well founded, be it on the basis of the fallen nature of humanity or on a reading of history. Accordingly, this suspicion should not be taken for ignorance or stupidity. There are grounds to doubt, based on experience, even if this is tentative in terms of what precisely might be the problem on this occasion. The suspicion might be quite general, and aimed at left and right, socialist and conservative. It might rather be a suspicion of all certainty, of the definitive, in politics, which suggests that there is only one answer and that only some have the means to find it. It is therefore the very opposite of the blimpish caricature of the reactionary. This sense of reaction refuses to accept certainty, rather than take a hard and prescriptive line. It sees the impossibility of taking any definitive position, which will lead us only to disappointment and possibly to disaster.

This may appear to be a form of anti-establishment radicalism, akin to those who challenge authority and wish to destroy current systems of authority. It might seem to be a form of nihilism, seeking to halt all forms of progress. Indeed this sense of reaction offers little that is positive. It offers no solution, no direction, and most definitely no programme of action. Instead of being nihilistic it might be better seen as fatalistic. It does not wish to destroy merely to persuade others that progress is an illusion. Accordingly, the reactionary does not seek to do anything other than to stand at the side and comment. It is an entirely negative position and it seeks to offer no political programme to reform the world away from where it currently is. But then neither is there any attempt to turn the clock back and to change things to how they once were. History goes in only one direction and we cannot put things back as they were and unlearn our cynicism. Things have gone wrong in the past and so long as we act things will go wrong in the future.

This poses us with two immediate problems. First, the reactionary remains a member of a particular community, and even though they may remain passive, they are already implicated in the activities of that community. They may be mere bystanders, but they remain a part of the society they criticise. They will not like or approve of it, but they will put up with it. They did not give their consent, but then it was not asked for, and an active refusal would have little impact other than personal humiliation. Reactionaries are products of the very societies they disdain. But most reactionaries are not unaware of this, and in consequence they can often see a knowing sense of contradiction: the reactionary recognises that they cannot live outside and beyond what they are critical of, and thus they are part of the very thing they anathematise. The fact that they can do no other might offer a partial comfort, but that is all. This sense of knowing merely adds to the fatalism of the reactionary, as it highlights the futility of any resistance.

The second problem is that the passivity of the reactionary may very well condemn them to irrelevance. If there is no political programme and call for change why should they be listened to? What have they to say that can influence anyone? What is the point of always saying 'no' without offering an alternative? There is the very real possibility that the reactionary, by not engaging, will leave the way open to the progressives and utopians. This indeed would seem to be the situation in the UK and USA, where there is no effective and active opposition to the ideas of progress and change. However, the alternative to this passivity would be to commit the very acts that one is condemning. It would be to suggest that progress and change is possible and perhaps even necessary. It would endorse the belief that they can plan the future with certainty. For the reactionary it would be to commit a wilful act of betrayal, worse than their apparent passivity, for example Oakeshott's critique of F.A. Hayek's 'plan to resist all planning'. As Callahan (2009) has argued:

> Oakeshott even accused F.A. Hayek, who might seem to be his natural ally, of responding to the proposals for improving society according to a 'rational' plan with a rationalist system of his own: 'This is, perhaps, the main significance of Hayek's *Road to Serfdom*—not the cogency of his doctrine, but the fact that it is a doctrine. A plan to resist all planning may be better than its opposite, but it belongs to the same style of politics,' he writes. (p. 25)

These are very real problems and they are difficult to contend with: we are all products of a particular culture and any withdrawal can only ever be partial. But the very act of withdrawal allows those who wish to ignore us the liberty to do so. But the reactionaries we will be relying on in this study have one very potent weapon at their disposal: their learning and their intellect. Their greatest asset is the very ability they have to eviscerate the modern world and to point to its follies and contradictions. They may be commenting on the sidelines, but their comments are substantial, weighty and worth listening to. Edmund Burke is no lightweight, and the same can be said for many of the thinkers we shall be engaging with in this study, whether it be Burke's contemporary Joseph De Maistre, or more modern thinkers such as Joseph Ratzinger and Roger Scruton.

This intellectualisation of reaction suggests that we should not confuse fatalism with quietude. These thinkers do not withdraw entirely in the sense of not wishing to argue for their point of view. However, they have chosen not to engage directly in political change. Instead these choose to write, to educate or to preach and to show that there is an alternative to the constant call for change. This form of reaction takes a very different form from that of Evola and his militant supporters who used bombing and assassination to try to make their point. It is also very different from modern mainstream conservatism, which accepts much of the jargon and approach of progressive politics and so joins in with the parade towards utopia (King, 2011).

Of course, the attitude we have been describing is a decidedly elitist one. It is outside the mainstream and scornful of the taken-for-granted attitude towards modernity and progress. It does not seek to build a mass membership to garner the support of the majority. This is because of an understanding that what makes a cultural tradition worthy of conservation is its complexity and depth, something which cannot be grasped by everyone. What is being argued for is difficult to articulate, and there is little obviously to be gained once it is articulated. The concern will therefore be to protect what is considered best within a culture, whether it be its art, language, literature and music or its sense of the sacred and the traditional. The withdrawal from active politics does not mean a withdrawal from life itself, and the joy for the reactionary is that there is so much beyond politics to provide solace.

III

But despite – or perhaps because of – their elitism, these reactionaries will realise that the suspicion that they themselves harbour is actually a deep-seated one shared by very many people. There is what we might term a commonsense form of this reactionary suspicion. It does not articulate itself as such, as a reaction against the modern world, although it does find much to object to. This common sense reaction tends instead to be piecemeal, where individuals react not because they see a general malaise or some pattern to which they object, but because of something specific. It might be a particular policy of government, or a single event that causes a reaction and a sense of disaffection. This feeling might be temporary and quickly dissipate or if might grow just as the Tea Party movement in the USA has grown (O'Hara, 2010).

This form of commonsense reaction can also be described as a form of withdrawal. It is where we refuse to engage and instead turn away from politics. It is quiet in the sense of an acceptance of the situation around us even as we complain of it. We know that there is not much that we can do to make any difference, and so along with our complaints goes a sense of impotence. We complain but without the readiness to challenge the way things currently are.

The views that are expressed as part of this form of reaction are entirely conventional. It is to adhere to the commonsense critique of politics and the ruling establishment. There is no originality here: indeed it is the very lack of originality – the fact that we all seem to agree – that is the strength of this position. We are not seeking to be unique, but the very opposite. We feel we are part of a majority who are excluded, not listened to and not appreciated by those who dictate the political and economic direction of the country.

This view can be articulated, and will be when the circumstances allow, as shown by the Tea Party movement in the US or the reaction to the parliamentary expenses scandal in the UK in 2009. But more frequently this sense of reaction does not coalesce around anything so specific. It is a commonsense reaction to a world that cannot be understood or controlled. There is no sense here of organised resistance, or of any movement to force change or to replace the establishment. Even with the parliamentary expenses scandal there was no mass movement, no uprising to replace those legislators who filled us with disgust. Instead most of the disaffected could be seen merely standing in the wings and shaking their heads in disbelief that things have turned out as they have.

On one level this might be seen as a form of acceptance instead of reaction. We do not seek change and so we have accepted the way in which we are governed and that the institutions that control and influence are all that there is and all there will be. But even though it does accept much of what is around us, it is a form of reaction in that we feel outside of the mainstream. We are excluded and ignored. Unlike the intellectual reactionaries, we do not seek to explain this or to diagnose the problems of modernity. Instead we seek to find some comfort from a world that we do not fully understand, and we do this by seeking common ground with those around us. We develop a discourse of apathetic resentment: we see much that is wrong, but not how to sort it out.

The intellectuals will write their books and comment pieces, and they might be read, at least by those already inclined to agree with them. Some of these intellectuals will make some attempts to engage in public discourse, albeit on their own terms. However, others, such as Davila, will withdraw to their libraries and resist any form of political engagement. This might mean that we can struggle ever to hear their voice. But this is not a problem with commonsense reaction, despite its impotence. We can readily hear these voices without going very far out of our way. When we buy a newspaper, queue for a bus or sit on a train we can hear this commonsense reaction. We can listen, and join in with those who are unhappy with the world, with the government and politicians in general, with those who are dismayed by multiculturalism and immigration, with welfare dependency or with the unreliability of the transport system. The activity of commonsense reaction, if we can call it that, is the voices all around us expressing their disquiet and disaffection with how the world is.

Most of us, most of the time, are busy just leading our lives. We do not, as a rule, dwell on what we want our society to be like. We do not tend to reflect on our country, and nor do we have a particular vision for it. We do not tend to consider how changes occurs and why. We have more practical matters to consider, such as paying the bills, bringing up our children and getting on with each other. But when we do reflect on these big issues we will only tend to do so in a rather negative manner. We are only forced to consider them when things go wrong, when they are not as we would like them to be. We do not often find the need to state what we think is right, and this is simply because we accept things the way they are and have come to expect. We might be able to state what we wish to keep — what is good about our lives — but perhaps not always why it is so good. Likewise, we may not have an accurate scale to measure how good or bad our situation really is. There are no means outside of ourselves to judge what makes our lives good or bad. And so, most of the time, we simply carry on, recognising only the problems, but putting up with them because that is what we do.

The prevalence of this view may well be due to particular circumstances in Britain at the start of the second decade of the 21st Century. It may be that this is one particular consequence of the financial crisis, recession and the parliamentary expenses scandal, all of which have tarnished the view of elites, be it politicians or bankers. There is certainly less tolerance of politicians and their doings. We perhaps do not automatically accept any longer that there are shared interests between leaders and led, or that authority is always legitimate. We are not, we think, 'in this together'. The effects of the recession, with the need to reduce public expenditure, might also have given stronger support to arguments about the negative incentives of welfare systems. It has made it harder to justify the structures that have developed to support low-income households, and this is because they cannot be so readily hidden and ignored. They are now part of the national discourse because of the concern about what government has done and is doing.

The basis of our communal life depends on acceptance and accommodation. We accept what we are and where we are. We have come to terms with our environment, and those around us, and so come to rely on particular habits, on particular roots and ruts that guide us and limit us to what we know and can understand (King, 2005). We are anchored, located, and given a direction by these roots and ruts. We find we need to accommodate ourselves to the ways of others, so that we fit together and find some sense of mutuality. This exists within couples, families, and within broader groups. It might involve formal rules – laws – as well as being dependent on conventions, norms and habits. We find a way of operating, a means of accommodating others and ourselves.

This means that we integrate our sense of disquiet into our established routines, and it is this that makes it a form of reaction. It is the means by which many of us come to terms with a world we have to operate within, but know we cannot control. In a way it becomes a form of comfort or of solace, where we can accommodate that which troubles us into our sense of the everyday.

IV

There is a distinction that needs to be made between these two forms of reaction. The intellectual form will be articulate and act according to principle. As we shall see, this involves a concerted critique of modernity and a defence of traditions, the sacred and the established. It is, we might say, a fully worked up form of antimodernism. However, the commonsense version we have begun to consider is in no way so articulate or certain. The idea of accommodating disquiet means bringing it into our normal lives, and we do not wish to throw off the comforts of the modern world. Our established way of life is within the modern world and includes all its comforts, whether it be the plasma TV, the PlayStation, broadband Internet, the iPhone and so on. And nor do we want the so-called high culture of the intellectuals. We do not read Eliot or Austen, but prefer *X Factor* and *Strictly Come Dancing*. As with other forms of reaction, the discontent is over politics and not towards all aspects of the culture around us. What this suggests, and this is an important limitation for reaction, is that the intellectual reactionary cannot rely on the commonsense reaction of the majority for support in their antimodernism. Much of what the antimodernist might object to is manifested in the popular culture of the majority. It may well be that the two interests coalesce, but there is no reason to assume that they ever will.

Commonsense reaction does not seek to change the world but merely shows a disaffection or sense of disquiet about how the world now is. This can be taken as a form of critique of the modern world, but it is not a rejection of it. It is a sense that we are not listened to, that we are ignored and have no control over the way things are. This might be seen as the resentment of an elite, and there is indeed something of this. But the more articulated form of reaction – whether it be from De Maistre, Guénon or Scruton – is most avowedly elitist in its approach to both politics and culture. This suggests that there are real differences between the two forms of reaction. However, what I hope to show in this discussion is that there are areas of commonality, and that the two views might be able to coalesce. I shall suggest that we ought to see the difference between them as one of articulation. It is the form and formality of the critique of the modern that differentiates these two views. This means that we will need to spend some part of our time on a discussion of modernity and how it has been manifested in the world of everyday things.

What I wish to show is that both forms of reaction can be quite simply summarised by a number of basic propositions. First, there is a general sense of disaffection and disquiet with aspects of the modern world, which will be more or less manifest depending on particular circumstances. Second, many people feel that they are not being listened to and that their views are of no account. If they are heard then their views will tend to be discounted as bigoted or ignorant. Third, many feel that their traditions and accepted ways of life are being threatened and changed without their direct consent and without seeking any agreement from them. Fourth, what might be seen as the 'establishment' – which, by definition, always excludes them – does not seem to have the same interests as they do. I want to suggest that these four elements are shared across different forms of reaction and can be used to unify the intellectual and commonsense responses to modernity.

Most of what we want is already here, and what concerns us is that we might lose some or all of this. What we want, I would suggest is simply to be left alone. We do not seek anything new. We do not appreciate progress, because it is something that we cannot understand and which, we fear, may actually exclude us. We do not want to be offered anything new: we merely wish to keep what we know. We have no need for new ideas. As Burke argued, in defence of the traditional values of England and in opposition to the new fangled ideas of the rights of man and the philosophy of Enlightenment:

> We know that *we* have made no discoveries, and we think that no discoveries are to be made, in morality; nor many in the great principles of government, nor in the ideas of liberty, which were understood long before we were born, altogether as well as they will be after the grave has heaped its mould upon our presumption, and the silent tomb shall have imposed its law on our pert loquacity. (Burke, 1999b, p. 181, original emphasis)

But, following Burke, we find that the case has to be continually remade, which is what we now set about to do.

Chapter Two

Reaction

I

To refer to someone as a reactionary is already to suggest that they are wrong. Reactionaries oppose reality. They are living in the past and refuse to accept the world as it is. Jean Starobinski, in his book on the developing usage of the words 'action' and 'reaction' quotes Victor Hugo's definition of reaction: 'a boat going upstream, which does not, however, prevent the river from flowing downstream' (Starobinski, 2003, p. 346). This is because, to amend slightly Sir Keith Joseph's dictum, the direction of the progressive ratchet cannot be reversed. The reactionary moves resolutely in one direction, but this has no impact on the world as it is. The river continues on flowing in one direction as the reactionary struggles heroically against the current.

Reaction is a word used to separate virtue from vice, truth from fiction, and rationality from sentiment. If conservatives argue against some reform they are reactionaries. But also the word is used against those who resist any form of change. Hence in 2011 the teaching unions in the UK were described as reactionary for opposing the government's proposals for introducing so called 'free' schools, outside of local authority control. As Starobinski states: 'In everyday language, 'reaction' designates what is against oneself' (p. 361).

Reaction is that which was once normal but that now we are no longer prepared to take as normal. It is the established rule we no longer wish to accept, the morality we can no longer abide. It is the refusal to accept the world as we now wish it to be. Accordingly, reaction is simply opposition, and as a result it is always unacceptable, always to be opposed. We now wish for a new 'normal' and so seek to demonise those who oppose the change, and use the term reaction to achieve this.

What this suggests is that reactionaries need not do anything to deserve the label other than stand still and watch the stream go past them. Some may be paddling upstream, but many might be sitting on the bank of the river watching it flow by. They do not enjoy their position, but feel that this is all they can do. Their primary concern is to preserve and protect what is in danger of being lost. This sense of realism means that the new is not simply rejected, but they consider how it might be assimilated without losing what they treasure most. Reactionaries know that the new will not go away, and that it cannot always be avoided. Therefore what matters is that, in assimilating the new, we do not destroy those things that we want to preserve. This is most assuredly a defensive position, and not completely at odds with the conservative disposition we have considered above. While there is a tendency to remain on the edge, this should not to be taken to mean that the reactionary will always remain on the outside. Reactionaries will engage in so far as they can maintain what we currently have and see as critical to our survival.

II

It might be useful, as a means of developing this idea of reaction, to consider briefly how the word 'reaction' has developed over time. The word has not maintained a steady meaning, but has shifted from a rather neutral sense, connected to causality – one action caused by another – to a concept that has overt political and cultural connotations. Jean Starobinski (2003) shows that before the middle of the 18th century the words 'progress' and 'reaction' were primarily value-neutral in their meaning.

At the start of the French Revolution the word 'reaction' had a meaning that 'was completely neutral' (p. 322). Starobinski states that it referred to 'the riposte, the action in the other direction, of a previously "oppressed" party or a cause under attack, whoever or whatever these may have been' (p. 322). He goes on: 'As long as the word maintained a neutral meaning, it was suited to designate abstractly any violence caused by previous violence' (p. 323). However, the partisans of the Revolution began to place their opponents as 'having only defensive or vengeful intentions' (p. 323). He

states that 'the emergence of the modern meaning of 'reaction' ... is linked to the advent of the idea of progress in political institutions' (p. 323). 'It was necessary', he states, ' to have a strictly delimited term to designate the action that goes against progress. (p. 323)
Starobinski argues that what helped to create this difference was the 'scientification' of politics and the social such that it came to be widely held that progress could be both achieved and measured. Starobinski argued that progress was associated with the idea of perfectibility, and, by definition, it was always good. Accordingly, what opposed - reaction - became seen as necessarily bad.

Instead of basing the temporal on sacred or providential notions the Enlightenment taught us to see human societies as entities capable of development and improvement. This progress could be quantified, such that we could be assured of its extent. A key element of this new view of social development was the Kantian notion of human perfectibility through the application of reason. By the use of reason we could determine the best form of society and it was the height of morality to seek to achieve this particular form. Progress, we can suggest, became to be seen as the application of reason. So instead of progress being a neutral term merely denoting a change, it became desirable in itself. But in turn, reaction came to be seen as the opposite of reason, as being based solely on the passions. Starobinski suggests that thinkers such as Benjamin Constant saw that 'A proportional equality is established in which revolution is to reaction what reason is to passion: reason is naturally at the service of political progress, whereas reaction can only be a matter of passion' (2003, pp. 333-4).

The effect of this was reaction became to be seen as entirely negative: it 'is a partisan word used only polemically or disparagingly' (Starobinski, 2003, p. 347). Furthermore, reaction became seen, often in hindsight, as a term with the specific meaning of a desperate and inevitable failure.

As politics became more about change and progress, and political leaders came to be measured by their ability to transform society, the greater became the need to discredit those who opposed change. The result was that the term 'reaction' was reduced to a form of abuse: 'One can categorise as reactionary those who embrace forms of politics that one wishes to discredit' (Starobinski, 2003, p. 351). This, Starobinski tells us, was not merely the preserve of the left, but became a generalised means of condemnation:

> Recall that in their use of force the tyrannies of the twentieth century all tried to pass themselves off as revolutions and that they sought, systematically or incidentally, to discredit their opponents by treating them as reactionaries. An abused word is often the first to be spoken. I will cite here only one example. The 'Horst-Wessel-Lied' – the war hymn of the German National Socialists – salutes the dead partisans: 'The comrades, shot down by the Red Front and the Reaction, march in spirit in our ranks'. Activism wants to be not a movement but a revolution, for being revolutionary means combating reaction, all the way to the ultimate sacrifice. (p. 352)

Reaction became to be seen as a generalised term of abuse, which can be applied by left and right to discredit their enemies. Reaction became a thing, an entity, hypostatised as the collection of regressive attitudes to the progress of civilisation.

This being so, should we not simply reject the word? Has it become so discredited, that we should turn to some other term to relate to those who wish to oppose progress but retain their respectability?

It is clearly the case, unlike the idea of progress, which is always seen as desirable, that many people who might be seen as reactionaries would shy away from acknowledging themselves as such. We can see why this might be when we consider a definition of reaction. It means to be opposed to what is perceived as radical change. While, in practice, this need not mean being against all change, as we have seen, many of the synonyms for the term imply precisely that: we find words such as blimpish, counter-revolutionary, die-hard, obscurantist and right-winger. It is unlikely that anyone would actively seek to be called either blimpish or an obscurantist.

We might suggest that the use of labels such as obscurantist and blimpish implies a sense of being outside of the mainstream and occupying some dark corner away from the normal flow of life. We are left with an image of the reactionary standing out against everything, their backs against the wall, seeking to hold off all and every change. But, of course, this is not what a reaction is at all. In science the word reaction actually means a change, and often a violent one. For a chemist a reaction is a response caused by a particular stimulus. Two compounds are introduced to each other and there is a reaction. This coming together of two different elements forces a response that leaves neither element in its previous state. The two elements react to form something new and different. An explosion, with all its consequences, is a reaction. So, in this sense, reaction is not about going backwards. As Starobinski (2003) has shown, it was once the case that reaction was seen simply as an action caused by an earlier action with no particular political value.

In the social and political sense we should therefore see a reaction as a causal response. It comes about in answer to some other phenomena. The aim of this reaction might be to stop something, to prevent an unwanted change, but this result might be a new and different social order that is an amalgam of the initial state and the attempt at progress.

However, the analogy with chemistry can only go so far. We cannot say that a chemical reaction is animated by any purpose. It happens because of the nature of the elements involved and their relative compatibility or incompatibility. But humans act for a reason and to achieve something. We do not respond automatically, although some of us might be more predisposed towards resisting change than others. However, whatever our predisposition, we have been provoked. The reason for the reaction is unlikely to be to create a new synthesis, but to stop anything changing at all.

This perception of reaction as backward and unthinking is only heightened when one looks at the meaning of 'progressive'. This is always seen as much more positive. It relates to the desirability and possibility of change and progress, and to the idea of moral and social improvement. This clearly suggests an optimistic view of human nature, and this is further emphasised by synonyms of progressive, which include avant-garde, dynamic, enlightened, forward-looking, go-ahead, liberal, modern, radical, reformist, revolutionary and up-and-coming. These different synonyms really show the judgmental manner in which each term is held. There is a presumption that progress is good, positive, virtuous even, whilst to be a reactionary is seen as largely negative and even absurd.

The progressive has the key advantage over the reactionary that the faults in their proposals are as yet unknown, whereas the problems of current and past arrangements are now all too clear. As yet we do not know what is wrong with specific attempts at reform and so one can only point to general problems such as unpredictability and the inevitability of unforeseen consequences. However, the progressive can point to specific problems that these reforms are set to tackle. They can be optimistic and portray the reactionary as pessimistic. And the great virtue for the progressive is that the situation is always moving on to new things and so they are seldom held to account for the consequences of their actions.

But, despite this, we might be able to point to a number of reasons for claiming the term in a more positive manner. First, it is sometimes the case that an individual or group will adopt a label applied to them by their opponents, as was the case with the US neoconservatives (Hielbrunn, 2008). So perhaps some might appreciate being known as a reactionary and take it as a term that describes them most accurately. If they are people who see themselves as reacting, as opposing all change and holding onto the present situation, then they might conclude it an appropriate term. Reacting is what they feel it is important to do. They see it as their role to stand at the side and to criticise; to cry out that the Emperor has no clothes; that what is being undertaken in the name of progress is not sophisticated, but a real risk, the consequences of which simply cannot be foretold. The greater the arrogance about the future direction, the more the reactionary is needed to calm things down.

This adoption of an ostensibly critical label, however, does not happen with any frequency, perhaps because, unlike the neoconservatives, who had a number of publications to promote their work, there is no organisation to act as a focal point for them. Reaction tends to be ad hoc and piecemeal, dependent on circumstance and so maintains no continuous focus.

Second, there may be those who are immune or protected from the flak of unfavourable opinion, either through wealth or position. There may be some people, such as royalty or those with extreme wealth or celebrity who feel that it does not matter how they are perceived by others and who can afford to call themselves by a label that has a particular resonance.

Third, we might term ourselves reactionary out of a sense of perversity or to be provocative. We do it in order to get a reaction. This might relate to a wish to connect with a particular historical association, but it might also be something of an affectation such as the so-called 'young fogeys', in their tweeds who frequented the old universities of England and Scotland of the 1970s and 1980s. The label of reactionary appeals to those who wish to make a particular statement that differentiates them from the prevailing modern world. There is also, without wishing to be overly trite, some utility in provoking a response in others at certain times. Some might wish to shake progressives out of their complacency and jolt them into explaining their call for change.

But both of these groups – the protected and the provocateurs – would still need to find some reason to defy public opinion. They might use the term reaction, then, because it is a term with a particular resonance. It has a history, whether it be the Counter-Enlightenment or those who fought the French Revolution and so the word takes on a particular appeal, it becomes a known term. It connects us to certain thinkers and ideas and so creates a sense of continuity. In our writings we might wish to be associated with thinkers of the stature of Burke and de Maistre. We might also suggest here an allied point to the two above, which is that using the term makes it clear just what it is that we are against: we oppose progress.

III

Reactionaries exist because of progress: because things keep changing and many, particularly those in positions of power, keep calling for change. Reaction, therefore, is a response to something concrete. It is against *something* and not just against all things. It is targeted and specific, the result of some event, or the fear of something. Hence Joseph de Maistre (1974, 1993) was not reacting against all and everything, but rather a particular set of changes brought about by the ideas of the *philosophes*, the Enlightenment, the French Revolution and the resulting regicide. The same applies to Edmund Burke (1999b, 1999c) who responded to the events in France, the consequent war in Europe and what he saw as the appeasing attitudes of the British government to the threat of French expansionism.

This reaction might, on certain occasions, appear to be radical and threaten as much change as the progressives and utopians. These reactionaries want to unmake, to pull down and then recreate. They seek a rather severe correction. So, for example, Mrs Thatcher referred to herself on occasion as both a radical and a revolutionary (Green, 2006) and President Reagan also sought to transform America. The Republicans in 1994 successfully sought a new contract with America seeking to transform the country. Sarah Palin, the defeated Republican vice-presidential candidate argued in February 2010 that it was time for a new revolution in America, this time against big government. Less recently, we can also point to the condemnation of the French Revolution undertaken by Edmund Burke (1992, 1999b, 1999c), although in this case he was comparing the stability of the English Constitution with the upheavals and bloody violence across the Channel.

What Burke suggests is that we can seek to be resilient and strong in the face of change, even where the sense of imminent danger is very great. Conservatives like Burke felt that the stakes were very high, in terms of the importance of the institutions they saw as being threatened. Were the ideas of the French Revolution to grow roots in England they might have strangled the indigenous ideas of hierarchy and order. So it matters to conservatives that change might have a fundamental or even ruinous impact on institutions seen as crucial to a particular way of life. In this way they feel that they must act, and act positively, in order to preserve what they see as threatened. Passivity and acceptance are not options once one's way of life is endangered.

Indeed, as we have already seen in chapter one, one of Burke's most famous phrases is 'A state without the means of some change is without the means of its conservation' (1999b, p. 108). Societies which cannot adapt will tend to ossify and die. They become brittle and fall to dust. Those societies which wish to survive, and to do so on their own terms, keeping their way of life intact, must be able to shift and roll with the changing tide of events. Change is not therefore to be rejected out of hand, but instead seen as a tool that has a very specific purpose, namely that of preservation. This then is not change for its own sake, but change for a limited purpose: it is change that does not seek to transgress, but to maintain. The purpose of change is not to improve or to progress, but to correct,[6] and so any action should be modelled on traditional forms that follow the grain of that culture. The means by which change should be engineered, Burke tells us, is by transplanting from the healthy parts of the Constitution and so change remains a part of our traditions rather than a departure from it. This is why Burke held such different attitudes to the revolutions in America and France, the former being 'not against the English constitution, but on behalf of it' (Wood, 1969, p. 44).

Burke would have us believe that any attempt at change should be seriously questioned. The reason for this is because, like Lord Salisbury, the great Conservative Prime Minister at the end of the 19th century, Burke had a somewhat pessimistic view of politics. Salisbury considered that it is easier to lose important things than to win them back or recreate them. We might call this the 'tightrope' view of politics. Experience tells us that there is only a very fine line along which we can travel and remain safe, and the consequences of moving off this line are disastrous and irreversible. It takes concentration, courage and fortitude and no little skill to retain our balance. We need to be extremely careful because we know that once we fall we cannot recover; once we have changed things such that once treasured institutions are gone they cannot be readily replaced or returned to. The old status quo cannot be rebuilt once it has been pulled apart – we cannot get back on the tightrope – and so our efforts should be put into preventing the changes from being made in the first place. This will involve us being strong-willed and determined to ignore siren calls that will break our concentration and lead to our downfall. The basis of Salisbury's philosophy of government could be summed up by the phrase 'delay is life' (Scruton, 2000, p. 197): our normal way of existing, and therefore of governing, is by a

---

6 One of Oakeshott's favourite texts was the Marquess of Halifax's *The Character of a Trimmer* (1688). According to Halifax's nautical metaphor the art of statesmanship is 'to keep the boat steady, while others attempted to weigh it down perilously on one side or the other'.

process of holding back change and protecting those institutions that maintain our way of life. According to Scruton:

> Salisbury was animated by the knowledge that it is easier to lose good things than to create them, and that the task of politics is to understand an inheritance of laws and institutions, and to protect it from unnecessary experiment. (p. 190)

This Burkean position recommends that we delay those forces that would destroy us and so allow our institutions to adapt and re-form in a manner that leaves them, and us, intact. The aim of politics is to remain safe, to survive so we can continue on. This might not be a gentle or even a consensual process, as Mrs Thatcher found when facing down trade unions and the left in the 1980s. This is precisely because events continue to occur, and so, as much as we might wish things to remain as they are, our way of life will from time to time come under threat and we must go out and fight for it.

The situation, however, was different for a thinker like Joseph de Maistre. He had lost all he held dear: the crown, the centrality of the church, his homeland and his birthright had all been taken from him (Lebrun, 1988). What he wanted therefore was not to preserve what existed in the present, but to return to what once was. He did not simply accept the status quo, but rather wished a radical transformation of it. This is because he saw this new state – revolutionary and imperial France – as illegitimate and against the natural order of things. Maistre was not reacting to the threat of change, but seeking instead to overturn change that had already occurred. He could therefore be seen as a counter-revolutionary.

John O'Hara (2010), in his book on the Tea-Party protests that began in reaction to President Obama's economic and health policies in 2009, draws a useful distinction between revolution and counter-revolution. O'Hara describes the US Tea Party protesters as counter-revolutionaries. They are fighting against a revolution they see as already underway and which is fundamentally transforming America, turning it from a country of individual freedom, low taxation and small government to a European-style social democracy. As O'Hara puts it, the protesters want their country back. They oppose the bailouts, health care reforms and cap and trade measures proposed by the Obama administration, seeing these policies as somehow alien to the American tradition. O'Hara portrays this as a genuine grassroots movement against what the protesters consider to be an over-large and over-active government. But what is particularly interesting is O'Hara's description of counter-revolution:

> [T]he movement is not and never was a revolution but a counter-revolution. This is a crucial distinction. To revolt is an attempt to break free from and overthrow a long-standing political structure. The tea parties do the opposite by opposing radical policies of bailouts, handouts, wealth re-distribution, and intrusion into our lives that can only be described as radically revolutionary. Big spending and a nanny state is radical. (2010, p. 203-4)

The tea party movement 'is about *protecting* individual liberty and the documents and institutions that have made it possible' (p. 204). He goes on:

> The tea parties and the movement they ignited aren't about a radical right-wing agenda but an American agenda. Our values are the values of the mainstream. The only radicalism involved in this movement is the preservation of the once radical ideas defended by the Founders that people should have a right to life, liberty and the pursuit of happiness. (p. 204)

So O'Hara argues that this movement is a concern to reassert mainstream values in the face of what is perceived of as an alien threat, as something deeply inimical to the political traditions of the USA. It is this assertion of being part of a threatened mainstream that leads de Maistre to qualify his views on revolution. He argued that his aim, the restoration of the monarchy in France, 'will not be a *contrary revolution*, but the *contrary of revolution* (1974, p.169). He is promoting the opposite of revolution, which seeks to restore what was long established but now lost. De Maistre proposes action in response to a previous action.

Of course, we need not accept this particular view. After all Barack Obama, who the Tea Party protesters are campaigning against, was elected with a clear majority. However, what does matter here is the self-perception of this group of ordinary people turned protesters. The Tea Party protesters do not see themselves as radicals or as revolutionaries. Instead they perceive themselves as working towards putting things back as they were. They are not seeking to preserve but to restore.

The Tea Party movement, like the two hundred year old arguments of de Maistre, are reactionary. They are seeking to counter something that is currently happening and which they profoundly dislike. We might see this protest as simplistic and negative. It tends to focus on what it is opposed to and perhaps sometimes taking for granted what it is for. They see the need to argue *against* rather than *for* something. The protesters are opposed to the current government and the so called 'beltway consensus'. Their main argument is to call for less of things or for them to stop outright rather than putting forward the stereotypical utopian dream of the revolutionary. Their anger is directed at change that has already occurred. So we can indeed see similarities here with the more neutral cause-and-effect argument of reaction that Starobinski (2003) identifies in pre-revolutionary times.

This suggests that reaction can take different forms: It can be defensive or active. What unites them is their attitude towards change, and that, in both cases, what is being attempted is not an innovation but a correction. Something, according to the reactionary, needs to be either prevented or put right and made good again.

What brings these two forms together are a number of common elements, which we might suggest are the basic points that most, if not all reactionaries will agree upon, whether they are concerned to protect or to restore. First, as we have seen they will be opposed to political and social progress. But second, they will argue along with Burke (1999b) that there can be no progress either in morality, that we do not have new things to learn, and that we cannot expect to improve our behaviour towards each other. This is because, Burke believed, our human nature is known and fixed. Third, we can state that there are certain proper notions of good and bad, and these can and should be applied to art, music and literature. We can distinguish between what is worthy and what is ephemeral. Fourth, reactionaries will argue that what has stood the test of time usually has done so for a reason which might make it worthwhile protecting further. There may be some utility in preserving that which has survived the rigours of continuous practice. This does not mean we should automatically reject what is new, but that we should recognise, as our fifth and final point, that what is new and good is often built on, or is a response to, what is old and good. A culture therefore should evolve rather than encourage any radical break with its past.

IV

Any action may cause a reaction. But this means that the very act of resistance can create change, as appears to be the case in the USA with the Tea Party movement's reaction to President Obama's policies. The intervention of the Tea Party movement has shifted political debate, led to the rejection of certain Republican candidates and changed the nature of political discourse in the US. Therefore a reaction might be both an attempt to pre-empt the consequences of change and itself the cause of further change.

This complicates our sense of what reaction might be and suggests that there is more to it than merely saying no. The result of reaction might be, for want of a better word, a progression. It might take a society into something new, which is unpredictable and uncertain. This, we might suggest, is not what a reactionary would necessarily be happy to have caused.

A possible way out of this dilemma is to suggest that instead of being against something, perhaps it would be better to take a neutral stance, to sit on the bank and watch. Instead of participation we should withdraw and refuse to take part. We should exile ourselves and take no part in the deliberations of our peers. This self-exile can clearly be portrayed as negative, or as apathy and a lack of interest. But perhaps neglect and drift are useful precisely because they are negative. We are not complacent in innovation and we have made no contribution to a worsening situation. There may be little for us to enjoy, but at least we do not compromise ourselves.

What we can hope is that this inaction will in some way balance those who presume that a change is always better than the status quo. It presents the proponents of change and innovation with a challenge and the result might be some compromise or diminution of the flow of change. In other words, and to return to our chemical analogy, we are seeking to create a controlled reaction. What we are seeking to do is to place a brake on change to ensure that we preserve what is important and do not lose it in a rush for what is new and untried.

As we have consistently stated, reactionary thinkers acknowledge that change is inevitable, but wish to ensure that its consequences are not too drastic and that no healthy flesh is removed along with the cancerous tissue. This might lead them to take action themselves in the hope that it is preferable to enact change oneself rather than their more adventurous opponents. As an example, Burke in his writings on Ireland, India and on slavery saw the need for reform and change, but only over time and in a controlled manner (Burke, 1999d). He put forward proposals leading towards the abolition of slavery, but he sought to do this in a way that did not completely overturn the social and economic arrangements of the time. This might be seen as delay for those who could not abide the iniquity of slavery, but Burke was concerned with what might come after slavery and how both former slaves and those dependent on the trade and its industries would cope with its abolition. Likewise, he argued that Catholics should be able to participate in Irish politics and elections, but not by tearing down those parts of the constitution which protected property rights and the established relations between the church, the state and its citizens. As Burke argued in defending the British constitution as it stood in 1782, despite its apparent lack of representativeness: 'It is for fear of losing the inestimable treasure we have, that I do not venture to game it out of my hands for the vain hope of improving it' (1999d, p. 30). He does not rule out change, but merely asks us to focus on what we might lose in rushing to deal with an apparent inequity. We should see Burke as attempting to devise a humane and sustainable situation that allowed change where it was needed but which preserved what deserved to be kept. This will certainly not satisfy the progressive, nor will it necessarily sound pleasing to one with 21st century sensibilities, but we should recognise that Burke was concerned with the attitudes and problems of his time. Burke wanted to ensure that we do not lose the good things in our rush to end the bad.

In more contemporary circumstances we should recognise that politicians tend to act incrementally, ensuring that they maintain popular support and take people along with them. This may mean that reform will be messy and open to compromise as circumstances change over time. It also might disconcert those who suggest that the government is not moving fast enough to deal with what are considered intolerable and unacceptable situations. However, we might suggest that we are more certain of arriving safely at our destination by taking many small and manageable steps rather than attempting one risky and dramatic leap.

So it is reasonable to argue that all politics is, to a greater or lesser extent, about reaction. Politicians must be pragmatic; they must react to the conditions they are presented with, and are forced to act within the considerable constraints of practical politics, where decisions cannot be readily undone and things in the public domain taken back.

But is there really no difference between being reactive, in the sense of having to respond to events, and being a reactionary? A reactionary, because they are set firmly on a particular path, might actually not react at all, but try to stay consistent, bent on achieving the general acceptance of their particular set of principles over and above every other condition. But this might also be the case with those overly besotted with progress, who put their plans over everything else. Examples might be Mao and Stalin, who respectively put their 'great leap forward' and five year plans above the realities of daily life and the actual conditions of their citizens. Even mass starvation did not cause them to alter their course. This rigid following of principle at the expense of all else is reminiscent of the caricature of the reactionary.

But we might just be confusing here a particular attitude with the consistency of purpose with which it is applied. There are some reactionaries who will hold out against all forms of modernity, just as there are progressives who are immune to caution and calculation. But we should not necessarily take these as demonstrative of their kind. As we have stated sufficiently often already, reactionaries are not opposed to all and every change, and likewise not many (if any) progressives take a fundamentalist 'year zero' approach to change. One can prefer reform to revolution, just as others might prefer negotiation to a fight to the death.

V

But this preparedness to compromise should not be taken to mean that reaction is mere expediency and has no connection to principle. We do not react on principle, but we do because of them. Thus we should not see reactionaries as being irrational, even if they are opposed to the particular rationalism of the French Enlightenment. Thinkers like Joseph de Maistre and Edmund Burke used reason to substantiate their opinions. They did not simply assert their opinions or flail about in anger, but instead sought to put forward a reasoned argument against particular changes or to call for a return to a previous situation. They presented arguments that were aimed at countering progressive opinion, and, because these were reasoned views, they themselves demanded clear reasoning if they were to be countered. Maistre, it is true, has been accused of fanaticism and madness (Berlin, 1990, Lebrun, 1988). However he was a highly cultured and learned intellectual who wrote in a particularly elegant prose style. He was certainly determined in his principles and so he might well be called, as Richard Lebrun (1988) does, an intellectual militant, but this takes nothing away from the quality of his thought. Burke, we might suggest, has been even more influential and frequently read, perhaps because he is more measured in his prose and his arguments. Burke, who might not have thought of himself as a reactionary (at least not until the very end of his life), is an entirely civilised thinker, and importantly, one who cultivated a coherent set of ideas and a political movement which is now referred to as conservatism (in the British and American sense). He was perhaps the first to achieve a consistent description of what we might see as modern conservatism and he did so in a manner that is both elegantly presented and intellectually consistent with the principles and disposition he seeks to detail. He offers no abstract theory, but provides a conservative approach to dealing with specific problems and issues and through this a means by which we can understand change and the need of a culture for its own traditions and history. Burke is able to explain how communities develop their own ways of operating and do so not by active design or on the basis of any individual action. Rather it is how actions meld together over time, given the freedom and space that continuity brings. As Burke tells us:

> ... a nation is not an idea only of local extent, and individual momentary aggregation, but it is an idea of continuity, which extends in time as well as in numbers, and in space. And this is a choice not of one day, or one set of people, not a tumultuary and giddy choice; it is a deliberate election of ages and of generations; it is a Constitution made by what is ten thousand times better than choice, it is made by the peculiar circumstances, occasions, tempers, dispositions, and moral, civil, and social habitudes of the people, which disclose themselves only in a long space of time. It is a vestment, which accommodates itself to the body. Nor is prescription of government formed upon blind unmeaning prejudices – for man is a most unwise, and most wise, being. The individual is foolish. The multitude for the moment, is foolish, when they act without deliberation; but the species is wise, and when time is given to it, as a species it almost always acts right. (Burke, 1999d, p. 21)

For Burke, it is accumulated wisdom that we should rely on rather than the current view or the opinion of the masses at any one point in time. We should see something as correct when it has stood the test of time and can therefore be relied upon. It is not just a passing vision or a momentary flash of apparent wisdom, but something which has been tested and found to retain its value.

Despite this it remains in the interests of the progressive to depict reactionaries as obscurantist, backward and unsophisticated, and to suggest that their reaction is a mere knee jerk or instinctive response to change that has no basis in reason or thought. It might well be the case that reactionaries come into their own when there is a strong sense of threat, when what they hold dear is perceived to be endangered. But, as a consequence, it is all too easy to associate reaction with negativity, with fear, dislike of the new, and hatred of the unknown and unfamiliar. Critics tend to use terms like 'horrified', 'disgust' and 'despised' with regard to how reactionaries apparently respond to ideas, as indeed Zeev Sternhell (2010) does when criticising anti-Enlightenment thinkers such as Burke, Johann Herder and de Maistre. Yet, in reality, these thinkers were much more positive and encouraging about their preferred systems. Where they reject change, they do so for sound reasons, which arise from their understanding of what we currently hold and what it would mean to lose it; about what certain institutions and traditions allow and why we should keep them. These thinkers revel in certain forms of social relations, which they see as uniquely beneficial, as being particularly tailored to certain ways of life. Accordingly, this way of life should not be cast off lightly.

Having said this, it is certainly the case that many of the arguments of reactionaries such as de Maistre can now be seen as wrong or out-dated, be it throne and altar (Maistre, 1850) or the inevitability of the executioner's role (Maistre, 1993). In this regard, Starobinski (2003) reminds us of Benjamin Constant's attitude towards political reaction. Constant saw it as a desire to return to the past and re-establish an earlier order. He equated this to homesickness and nostalgia. He linked reaction to the passions, to a sentimental yearning for things of the past. The reactionary, whose happiness has gone, seeks to restore it and to recreate the source of that happiness, even if in doing so he also needs to re-create old inconveniences and abuses. The past becomes something that is complete where the sought-after cannot be separated from the abuses.

This being so, why should we still read de Maistre? Partly, it is because he is a great prose stylist, and partly because it is important to understand our intellectual antecedents. We read many figures from the past to understand our present, and this includes even those who might be said to have ended up on the losing side. I want to suggest that there are sound reasons for reading de Maistre apart from the sophistication of his argument. In particular he reminds us of the limitations of what it is to be human. De Maistre places us within a greater scheme than of our own making and understanding, and so calls into question the human quest for perfection. De Maistre was sceptical of science and of what we now refer to as positivism and argued instead for a return to a more providential view of human social order (Maistre, 1993, 1998). There is very little we can do on our own in a more complex world not of our own making. As Starobinski says of de Maistre:

> One needed only to be patient. In the meantime, the Jacobins and the republican armies would do their work – territorial conquests – that would eventually profit the future monarchy.

> The designs of Providence would be realized with the inevitability of the laws of nature (2003, p. 327)

De Maistre demonstrates a particular cast of mind, a mentality that is properly reactionary. He is one of the best examples of a brilliant and cultured mind turned to maintaining a particular traditional sense of the world. De Maistre's virtue is in his attempt to show the unvarnished reality of human nature, and so to provide a necessary counterweight to Enlightenment optimism and the idea that progress was inevitable. He shows us that progress can be destructive, and this is because of how human beings really are rather than what the French *philosophes* assumed them to be. Human beings, according to de Maistre, need order, discipline, constraint and punishment. He reminds us that wars happen and that some people relish them and are proficient in prosecuting them, and that the rest of us rely on these people for our protection. We are glad when such people are there for us, even as we might be concerned about what they actually do in our name and we might not wish to delve too deeply into the full nature of their actions. In short, de Maistre shows that human beings are by no means perfect, nor are they perfectible, and this is not just some temporary aberration.

VI

So we are beginning to establish that reaction need not be unthinking. Indeed, what the reactionary seeks to protect is by no means narrow and parochial. As Scruton (2007) shows, the culture that modern reactionaries try to defend, what might be called Western civilisation, is based on broad principles, and is not, of course, merely the product of one culture:

> Civilisations grow out of and into each other, and often divide like amoebas so as to generate two contemporaneous offshoots; hence, it is very hard to set spatial or temporal boundaries on Western Civilisation. It grew from the fusion of Christianity with the law and government of Rome, became conscious of itself in the high Middle Ages, passed through a period of scepticism and Enlightenment, and was simultaneously spread around the globe by the trading and colonial interests of its more adventurous members. And throughout its most flourishing periods, Western Civilisation has produced a culture which

> rapidly absorbs and adapts the cultures of other places, other faiths and other times. Its basic fund of stories, its moral precepts, and its religious imagery comes from the Hebrew Bible and the Greek New Testament. Onto those Judeo-Christian roots, however, has been grafted a tree of many branches, bearing many kinds of fruit. *The Thousand and One Nights*, which has a central place in Islamic culture, is equally part of the cultural heritage of the West, while the pagan literature of Greece and Rome has been taught for centuries as the fount of our literary tradition (2007, p. 3)

This civilisation, therefore, is not a product of insularity, but its very opposite. It is the result of an outward-looking search based on the wonder of things around us. What reactionaries seek to protect therefore is not just the result of a narrow inward-looking process but something that is positively global and which has been built up over centuries. As Scruton argues: 'it is important to understand, in the context of today's "culture wars" and the widespread advocacy of "multiculturalism", that Western culture has an unparalleled ability and willingness to assimilate other cultural traditions' (2007, p. 4).

What is being threatened therefore is not something based on just one culture but which has a wide base and is the product of thousands of years and possibly millions of minds. However, this does not stop the threat to it, and much of Scruton's endeavours has been in defending Western civilisation from threats from the inside, from what he terms a culture of repudiation, which seeks to undermine the very basis of the western tradition. As a result his view tends to be somewhat elegiac. He is concerned with the loss of much of our culture and so his writing is tinged with a pessimistic sense that we may already be too late to save our own heritage. This view is shared by Joseph Ratzinger and Marcello Pera (2006) in their discussion of how Western civilisation now appears increasingly to be 'without roots'. They argue against the intellectual dominance of relativism, post-modernity and the idea of progress. Ratzinger and Pera state that in Europe and elsewhere we have a culture that is based on a clear history with its roots in Athens and Jerusalem. We are part of a Greek and Judeo-Christian tradition which we risk compromising by our accommodation to other ideas such as liberal multiculturalism. They portray

Europe and America as tearing themselves apart from the inside through a philosophy and politics of disenchantment and alienation. Many in the West have become embarrassed and even ashamed of their own culture and history and seek to replace it with something else. But the result, as many conservatives and reactionaries would argue, is not actually to replace one culture with another that is equally valid, but to leave a gaping hole, a void where nothing of significance is left.

We might see the desire for change, then, as a form of self-loathing, as a sense that we no longer approve of, or even like ourselves and the culture we have made. Instead, as Roger Scruton (2006, 2010) has argued, we seek to repudiate our culture, to negate it, to destroy it. We focus on how it has failed, what it has wrong, its lack of legitimacy, and not on what it has achieved.

But is our culture – the very one that permits dissent, argument and difference and provides the leisure to question – really so bad? Instead, might we not see that there is much left to celebrate in Western culture and it is by no means all lost? Much of what Scruton, for instance, loves still exists to be uncovered and celebrated. In his works on aesthetics he is able to present a particular vision that maintains traditional virtues and the notion of the beautiful (Scruton, 1994, 2009). A particularly fine example is his essay entitled 'Eliot and conservatism' (Scruton, 2006). This is a profound and quite beautiful description of what is worth preserving in our own culture, based on an acute reading of T S Eliot's poetry and his understanding of the meaning of culture. It is inspiring and affirming, and the very opposite of the hysterical and declamatory sense that reactionaries are often accused of deploying. He shows how Eliot is capable of mixing the rhythms of ordinary speech with the great traditions of European poetry. Eliot re-shaped the English language by bringing together the old and the new and in doing so he did not repudiate or seek to alienate as is common with modernist art, but to affirm the modern precisely by its connection, its very symbiosis, with the past. Scruton is here not arguing against anything, but seeking to explain what we actually still have and why we might still need it. He is telling us how it can remain alive. Scruton, as in much of his writing, is here arguing *for* something and he is not merely an opponent of all that is new and untried. For him, there is enough in what we already have that remains available to us if only we would take the time to look.

It is therefore a mistake to equate reaction with backwardness or an uninformed view of the world. It may be that what motivates some reaction is fear, but it is often more considered than this. Or at least for reactionaries, there is every reason for them to fear for the loss of certain irreplaceable things.

VII

Often we will find that reactionaries are rather worldlier than progressives, lacking, as they do, the latter's obsession with utopian abstraction. As the examples of Burke and de Maistre show, the reactionary is very much within the world. It is not necessarily the case that reaction leads to a fatalistic attitude. One view of reaction can indeed lead to the conclusion that we should accept our fate and not seek to change anything. If we cannot predict the outcomes of change we should not accept any of it and so just take the consequences of being where we are. But fatalism might actually be inconsistent with reaction, in that to be fatalistic is to accept change as it happens rather than to reject or argue against it. Fatalism is not about accepting the status quo and fighting for it, but simply standing idle and doing nothing to protect what we hold dear. It is to be passive and to accept all change without any attempt to mitigate or prevent it. The fatalist accepts life on another's terms, and this is not acceptable to reactionaries who tend to know what they want and desire to keep it. Therefore reactionaries cannot be entirely fatalistic or disengaged. De Maistre certainly believed in providence, but this did not lead him to quietism, even if he might appear to have advocated it. Indeed if he had been really so quiet he would not have seen the need to espouse providentialism which such fervour and eloquence. De Maistre wrote, educated others, and argued for what he believed in. He was not a revolutionary, but nor was he idle. He argued that the terror should take its course, because providence dictates that it would ultimately fail.

This raises the issue of how far one can be a reactionary and active in politics. If we seek something beyond or outside of what currently exists, where the mainstream demands progress and change, then how far can a reactionary take part. As we saw in chapter one, there are some thinkers, such as Nicolas Gomez Davila, who have suggested that we should restrict ourselves merely to spreading scepticism and suspicion from the comfort of our study. But will this be sufficiently satisfying for those who have a vision for their community, or for those who have such a sense of loss? But Davila was not himself always quiet: he merely did not seek to involve himself directly in politics. Like de Maistre, he indulged in dialogue and comment. He left active politics to others perhaps, but did not seek to limit his own influence through other media.

Indeed, if we accept the world as it is, we have no option but to engage in the world on the only terms that are offered. We may have some choice in how we engage and in what manner, but we cannot set the rules ourselves. This may open up reactionaries to claims of inconsistency, but in this regard they are no different from any others who engage with the world as it is while seeking to change or correct it. It may be the case that reaction is seen as cynical and that it cannot offer anything positive. Reactionaries might not seek to add to a debate: they might not wish to build anything, but rather to destroy, to tear down. Of course, this forgets that progressives may not actually know precisely what it is they are trying to build, what it will look like, what it will cost, or even if it will stand. Yet this will often be taken as a better stance than being negative. At least, it is argued, the progressive is offering hope, while all the reactionary can bring is cynicism.

This brings us to the question of how much compromise we can accept and remain a reactionary. We can suggest that we ought to accept a degree of compromise where this might best preserve the past. Compromise might be the best way of maintaining some of what we have, but to do so we have to give something away and this will be displeasing to some reactionaries. Accordingly, we face the problem of how far we allow ourselves to respond — or react — to circumstance. As we have suggested, much of politics is a reaction to circumstance, but this will involve compromise with progress and so perhaps leads us into acting in a non-traditional manner. The difference here is whether we react in a purely circumstantial manner, or whether we react because our principles dictate. Only the latter is seen as reaction in conventional terms, whilst the former is merely a form of pragmatism. This is by no means undesirable, and might be the only form of reaction that is really tenable in a democratic society so set on the idea of progress.

A more serious criticism of reaction is that it is bound to lose. As change always occurs, and it is only ever possible to delay or mitigate its effects, reactionaries are certain eventually to lose any battle they seek to join. It is certainly the case that we can view the history of the last two centuries as one progressive victory after another. This might suggest that reactionaries have not been particularly effective in holding back change. However, the situation is rather more complicated than this. It is precisely because reactionaries tend to lose that they still exist. If they were to win, assuming that we could decide what 'to win' might mean, and that all reactionaries could agree on this definition, this would put reactionaries out of business. The very reason that there are reactionaries is because of the persistence of the call for progress. There would be no need for reactionaries were it not for progress.

So, ironically, it is fortunate for the future of reaction that progress is always presumed to be the default position. Progressives always see current arrangements as contingent and continually look to make further changes: utopia is always just in front of us, only slightly out of reach. Progressives always seem to be needed and have a lot of work to do, and, in turn, they ensure that reaction is always needed.

What makes reaction particularly necessary is that progressives nearly always fail to deliver what they proclaim is inevitable. Reaction is a natural consequence of the failure of progressives and utopians, and it remains in existence because of the inability or refusal of progressives and utopians to learn.

Progress is always prey to unintended or unforeseen consequences and unpredictability. Reactionaries are able to state with a high degree of certainty that things will go wrong. They may be unable to be specific and to say exactly what will go wrong, but it will be clear to them that things never go as planned and that much of the optimism of progressives is ill-founded. It is reasonable to state that progressives will misunderstand things, and that mistakes will be made by them. No one can understand every nuance and calculate every eventuality. This suggests that the reactionary's response is rooted in empirical evidence. It is based on the actual experience of the implementation of change. The fact that reactionaries tend to lose therefore only makes their view of the world more necessary and ensures that there is a place for reactionary thought. They can rely on the simple fact that progressives never learn.

We might state, therefore, that reactionary thought is the concrete statement of the actuality of practical politics. It is a statement of what really does occur rather than relying on what ought to be. Perhaps we should argue, without undue cynicism, that the jargon of progress is underpinned by the realisation of the need and preparedness to react to changing circumstances in order to preserve our aims and intentions. Philosophers of a Hegelian bent like to see the progressive and reactionary vectors as necessary as the accelerator and brake pedal on a vehicle. Oakeshott (2004, p. 182), introduced a third pedal, the 'scrotch peg' – fitted on the Sussex farm wagon (c.1924) to prevent it running backwards down a hill. This, according to Oakeshott, was the chief function of social conventions.

But this gives thoughtful reactionaries only a little comfort: the best they ever achieve is mitigation of the aims of the progressive. This might explain the elegiac nature we have already found in some conservative thought. English conservatives, like Scruton (2000, 2007, 2009), look back and see that much is now lost, and so the best they can do is to remember it before it is all forgotten. There is little in the way of anger or cynicism in this writing, just a sense perhaps of being let down, almost of the childishness and superficiality of progressives who toss away so much in their vain attempts to create a better tomorrow, whether it is in art, architecture, education or politics. The elegiac quality is because conservatives know that things could have been different, that we did know better but somehow allowed ourselves to be led along a potentially destructive route from which we cannot now return. We had the culture, the institutions and the enlightenment to prevent much of the changes that we now regret. But we did not do enough to stop the destructive changes. This might lead to anger, but equally it may create a strong sense of regret and an equally strong desire to hold on to what appears to be fading.

This situation is perhaps an inevitable consequence of living in the present and with what we have now. We do not spend our time plotting and planning, and we are not seeking to control institutions and determine political action. We are busy elsewhere and so we leave the future to those who have a vision and a purpose and the drive to implement it. The conservative instead does not see the need to be continually questioning or justifying their place in the world. However, this attitude, as Richard Lebrun writes in his biography of Joseph de Maistre, presents a problem for the reactionary intellectual:

> Much of the strength of a traditional society lies in the fact that its structure and values are unquestioned – indeed unquestionable. It is only when the status quo has been attacked and disrupted that the need to defend it becomes imperative. The conservative theorist almost inevitably finds himself in a defensive posture, involved in a debate on the relative merits of the old order versus the new, impelled to base his arguments on the assumptions of the innovators. And by engaging in the argument at all, he easily becomes suspect to members of the traditional elite who have always simply assumed the rightness of existing structures and values and their own privileged place in the traditional order. (Lebrun, 1988, p. 124)

As de Maistre himself stated in *Against Rousseau* (1996, p. 86): 'If a belief is not attacked, it would be useless to declare it'. Our beliefs only need expression when they are challenged, otherwise we could carry on without their articulation. Our beliefs become precious when they are attacked and we can no longer take them for granted. We are immersed in our world and do not recognise the importance of our way of life until it is under threat. Once our views are attacked we start to see them as distinct entities, as elements separate from us, yet very important, even crucial to us. They stop being merely part of us, or things just as they are, and instead become a distinct set of principles that need articulation in order to mount a defence. They have a meaning and a history. The principles become part of public discourse instead of being merely inchoate. We have to recognise what we have and what it means to us, and the threat of their loss makes this all too clear to us. We can no longer be complacent and our conservatism slips into reaction.

The danger, of course, is that we do not recognise what is being threatened until it is too late. And, as Lebrun (1988) pointed out, even if we shout 'fire' we may not be thanked by those who are still to have their complacency disabused. The conservative might not wish to listen to the reactionary and will certainly need some convincing before he is prepared to join them in either battle or exile. The result is that we might find ourselves excluded, as prophets without honour in our own land, unable to make our neighbours listen to us.

VIII

There are two final issues that I wish to deal with before moving on to look at a different form of reaction. They will become important to us later as they open up the nature of reaction and show what is at stake when we seek to address modernism. These two issues are the attitude reactionaries have towards capitalism, and secondly, whether there is an unbridgeable difference between the two main forms of reaction in the modern world: what we might define as *Old European* and *Islamic* reaction.

There is the need for caution in trying to categorise reaction too readily. One particularly important example of this is the attitude of reactionaries towards capitalism. We might best describe this attitude as ambivalence. Some might see capitalism as the least-worst option, it being better than any other possible form of social and economic organisation. Others might be more positive seeing capitalism as the best protection of private property, individual rights, and the rule of law. But reactionaries have found much that is wrong with capitalism. In particular, capitalism can be seen as destructive of tradition. It places innovation above the tried and tested and puts a higher premium on profitability and efficiency rather than what is traditional. For many reactionaries the very idea of creative destruction will seem appalling. Accordingly, we can point to many critics of 19th century capitalism, such as Thomas Carlyle and John Henry Newman. For much of the 19th century, the Conservatives' predecessors, the Tories, were an agrarian, anti-urban and anti-industry party. They were the party of the country and were not associated with free markets and liberalism until well into the 20th century. As Ramsden (1988) shows, the splits in the Tories, whether over the Corn Laws in the mid 19th century or Imperial Preference in early 20th century, were precisely over whether government should give the market free rein. More contemporary conservatives such as Roger Scruton (2001) make the point that there is no necessary connection between capitalism and conservatism, and do so precisely because of its effect on longstanding institutions.

An interesting example of a contemporary reactionary is the Prince of Wales (2010), who is highly critical of materialism and many aspects of modernism. He is critical of industrialised agriculture and modern architecture. As we shall see in chapter four, the Prince has argued for some form of harmony between the human and natural worlds. He is highly sceptical of human progress, placing a higher premium on ecology and a sustainable relationship with the planet than on material progress.

As we shall see the Prince has been influenced by what has become known as perennialism or traditionalism (Sedgwick, 2004). This is the idea that there is a primordial transcendent tradition that underpins all the ancient religious and philosophical systems of the world. What makes this view important for our discussion on reaction is that, like the Prince of Wales, it provides a critique of modernism grounded in a reactionary worldview. The preeminent perennialist, René Guénon (2001a, 2001b) has argued against the materialism of the modern world. He is critical of the emphasis that modernism places on quantity as opposed to quality. Guénon is critical of the materialism of the modern world, with its focus on technology and modern science and neglect of the traditional and the spiritual. In place of modern capitalism, Guénon (2001c, 2001d) proposes a traditionalist, elitist society in which the spiritual is privileged over temporal authority and what he calls 'traditional sciences' supplant materialism.

We shall discuss these issues more fully in chapter four, but we can see this implies that there is no necessary connection between reaction and capitalism. There is no vested interest on the part of reactionaries to protect a particular economic system, especially one that promises the innovation and the destruction of traditional forms. However, it might be the case that currently, and over the last 100 years, there has been more serious threats than that presented by capitalism. In comparison to communism and fascism we can see capitalism as relatively benign and offering a degree of protection from the predations of authoritarianism. Capitalism, whatever faults it may have, has no death camps or genocides. Reactionaries might therefore have some reason to prefer capitalism to other forms of economic organisation: it may indeed be the least-worst form of economic and social organisation.

Yet there are some forms of reaction that are thoroughly out of sympathy with any form of modernity. In particular, we can think of political Islam. This is not only highly critical of capitalism, but also rejects modern democracy, human rights and the placing of temporal authority above the spiritual. But can we see political Islam as reactionary in the manner that we have been discussing here? In its critique of modernity political Islam certainly seems to be a form of reaction. But, on the other hand, it is also seeking quite fundamental change and of a form that is not a correction or a return to a former status. This form of Islam seeks to re-establish the Caliphate, and to extend it across the entire world. While the possibility of the crescent flag flying over the White House may not be anything near realistic, it is not a call for the status quo. It is rather a dramatic and radical proposition, even a call for a revolution. This is not really about restoration, but rather a utopian argument that, in its more extreme forms, is quite happy to use terror and violence to achieve the changes it desires.

So, even though political Islam has clear reactionary tendencies it does not seem to fit well within a European conception of reaction. As we shall in chapter four, the forms of traditional life that Europeans seek to preserve are not those of Islam. Indeed, it is quite possible to argue that many Europeans will see the growth of Islam in Europe as the greatest problem they face (Fallaci, 2002, 2006). Of course, we would not expect that all reactionaries will agree, nor are all those who are called reactionary in fact are so (and perhaps some who won't accept the label actually are). But, as we have suggested, Islamic fundamentalism might not actually be reactionary in the manner in which Europeans would accept, and what these Europeans actually wish to preserve, some Islamists might actually see as the problem to be remedied. Islamists, therefore, might have more in common with utopians and revolutionaries and are prepared to use similar methods in achieving them.

This leads us to an important point about the nature of 'European' reaction as we have described it. This form of reaction might show a degree of anger at times, but it is seldom if ever violent. Indeed, it is more likely to withdraw, to go into exile, than to lash out in anger. It therefore takes a very different form from other forms of reaction we can identify. Likewise, European reaction is unlikely to be systematic, but rather to be more specific and based on particular issues. Reactionaries might call for the restoration of a particular institution, or the repeal of a specific measure. Hence many opponents of the revolution in France called for a restoration of the monarchy (de Maistre, 1974). But it will be more common for the reactionary to put a brake on change than to seek to move backwards. There will not be much of a clamour for change, in the knowledge that history moves only in one direction and that we cannot unlearn what we know of the world.

Accordingly, reactionaries will not tend to have grand plans for long-term change. They will find the very idea of revolution distasteful and will instead fear it, seeking to place what is known and established over what is new. This means that they will tend to be negative rather than positive, to reject rather than accept change and to find arguments against rather than in favour of change. They will look inwards rather than outwards. They will be nostalgic, but without being overly sentimental. They will look close to them to find a home and once they have found it seek to maintain it.

But whatever the differences in forms of reaction we can see one issue that they will have in common. European and Islamic reaction may not agree on what they wish to change or preserve, but they will agree that the problem is what they term modernism. It is the modern world that reactionaries object to and it is what they are therefore against. It is clearly not the case that there is a natural affinity between all reactionaries: they do not coalesce merely because they are reactionaries. But they do agree that they are against the modern world, and this may therefore help us to a fuller understanding of reaction.

However, before turning to the reaction to modernity in an explicit way I wish to explore a further form of reaction. This is a form that is less overt and less articulate. It is not necessarily based on a set of articulated principles, but rather on a commonsense view of what is wrong with the world in which we live. This discussion will both extend and complicate our understanding of reaction and its impact. However, as we shall see as the argument develops, it will also mean that we can come to terms with just how thoroughly reaction is embedded in a culture.

Chapter Three

Common Sense

I

Politics is about speech and action. It can be very loud, with opinions stated in a strident and uncompromising manner. People who are involved in politics will tend to have strong opinions and they will have invested much in their own rectitude. They believe they are right and that their opponents are wrong, and they wish to make both of these points very clear. The result of this is often a cacophony, with activists seeking to outdo their opponents and be heard.

There is also a tendency to give more credence to those who shout the loudest. They are the ones we hear most readily and so we might think that these views are the most significant. However, Edmund Burke reminds us that this is not always the case:

> Because half a dozen grasshoppers under a fern make the field ring with their importunate chink, whilst thousands of great cattle, reposed beneath the shadow of the British oak, chew the cud and are silent, pray do not imagine, that those who make the noise are the only inhabitants of the field; that, of course, they are many in number; or that, after all, they are other than the little shrivelled, meagre, hopping, though loud and troublesome insects of the hour. (1999b, p. 180)

There may be a cacophony created by a few active creatures and we can perhaps believe that this relatively small number of noisy individuals is all that there is in the field. But this would mean ignoring a much larger number of more significant creatures that are silently going about their business. They are not shouting, but instead are just sitting unobtrusively ignoring the clamour around them. For them, all this noise is of no import.

Burke's point was that those who make the loudest noise, in his case the British supporters of the French Revolution, are not the majority and their voices are not the most significant, even if they might be hard to ignore and grab much of the attention. For Burke, the majority of those in the country did not support revolution or wish to import it into their own country. Instead they were content to let things carry on with their lives as normal, ignoring the rather vacuous noise around them.

Most of us, most of the time, are not active in politics. We might vote, but we do not wish to be active in the sense of attending meetings, becoming active in a party or a campaign, or even involving ourselves in political debate. As Oscar Wilde is reputed to have said, 'The trouble with Socialism is that it takes up too many evenings', and we have so many other more important things to do. Of course, at election times we take an interest, and do this because we know that it is important. But, by the same token, we do not believe it matters above all else or that it is a matter of life or death. So we vote and do so to ensure that we have politicians who will do things on our behalf, which will then allow us to get on with what we consider to be more important.

But even though we sit back and take a rather passive stance, we still expect politicians to act on our behalf. We expect that, amidst their chatter, they do not forget who they represent and what they have been put in office to do. We reserve the right to criticise and complain once the politicians do not act in the manner expected of them.

In some ways this seems to be an unreasonable position for us to take. We do not wish to be active ourselves, but we reserve the right to criticise those elected to represent us. We want politicians to do things for us and if they do not do this we will complain, but still without feeling the need to get involved any further ourselves. We restrict our involvement to the occasional vote and the continual moan.

This position, which I take to be reasonably common, is a form of reaction. It is not one that is so overt as that of thinkers such as Burke, de Maistre or Scruton. It is not articulate and is not based on any set of principles. It is not even a position that would necessarily recognise itself as reaction. Many of those who act in this manner might consider themselves to be in favour of progress and they would not refuse much of what the modern world has to offer in terms of its technology and amenities. As much as we complain about our politicians and wish that they would do better, we do not want to do without our comforts. The manner in which we gain our information on politics and develop our views is through the modern media, and we may use it to express our discontent, all the while sitting amidst the comforts of the modern world.

This is an argument that will need some justification if it is to be accepted. However, I wish to show that there is a form of commonsense reaction, and that this is a rather pervasive view. It is indeed inchoate and difficult to articulate, but it is a view that we need to appreciate and come to terms with. Politics in many parts of the world can be characterised by disquiet and disaffection. This has taken the form of direct action in places such as Greece since 2010 and in parts of North Africa in 2011. Likewise, the more sedate and respectable acts of the Tea Party movement in the USA can be seen as an example of disaffection with contemporary politics and the direction in which the country is heading. But there are many more examples of this subdued form of disquiet, such as the anger caused by the financial crisis in 2008 and the role of the banking system in its near collapse, the hostility towards British parliamentarians over their expenses in 2009 and the growing concern over corruption and the lack of accountability of French politicians.

In these more subdued forms in Europe the clamour was not for a change of government, but for a change of attitude on the part of politicians. In both the UK and US, where elections were held in 2010, there was a shift representative of this disaffection, but nothing that could be stated as decisive. The Labour Government in the UK was ousted, but without another party being given a majority, and while the Democrats lost considerable support in the US they did not lose control of the Senate. The respective electorates wanted their politicians to behave differently and to be more responsive and responsible. However, they did not want to rule themselves and so had no alternative but to elect – and re-elect – politicians to act for them. The level of disaffection caused by the events since 2008 were considered serious, but the response remained at a relatively low level and did not breach the sense of legitimacy that was contained in the prevailing structures of government. Electors still accepted the form of government that had developed over time and which they felt still served them satisfactorily enough. What they felt was that they were not being listened to, that politicians were getting away with too much. As a result they wanted the politicians to listen and to act differently.

I see this as a common sense form of reaction. It is not one that is actively articulated and which cannot be expressed in terms of concrete principles. However, it is a pervasive view, which colours much of politics, and which needs to be understood more fully.

II

We get annoyed with politicians. We feel they let us down. They fail to live up to their promises. But we not do wish to manage without them.

Despite their faults we do not expect them to do anything other than what they have always done: we want them to take decisions and to act on our behalf. We do not see it as our role to change things: that is what we elect politicians for. So we expect them to do the changing even as we consider them to be the cause of our problems. We may feel that they are all the same, but all we seek to do is to replace one set of politicians for another, whilst telling anyone who will listen that they are all alike and only in it for themselves.

The only alternative we might consider, which we are apparently doing in ever larger numbers, is to abstain from voting, perhaps thinking vainly that this will teach them a lesson. But this merely means that others do the job of picking the politicians without consulting us, and we still bear the consequences and costs of these and subsequent decisions as if we had voted. We might try to claim that it had nothing to do with us, but this makes no difference and we are as affected as if we had actively chosen the new government. Not voting does not help us avoid the decisions made by politicians, even if we might get some small comfort from not feeling directly responsible. We still have to pay our taxes, use public transport, schools, hospitals and so on. Our abstention has not materially weakened the government or made it less legitimate. All we have done is allowed the politicians to get on with pursuing their aims and, because we have opted out, we cannot hope to influence them.

Of course, despite our grumbling most of the time, in the US and Europe at least, the stakes are reasonably low. Politicians are indeed all the same, in that generally, with only a few exceptions, they tend to abide by the constitution and traditions of the country, and they do not break the law (or are liable if they do). The politicians, generally speaking, ignore us too and allow us just to get on with our lives. We can suggest that stability breeds stability and complacency more of the same too. Politicians get away with what we let them and we want to give them a lot of leeway because this frees us up to do what we think is more important.

But there is a consequence of this easy-going complacency. Those who are not active in politics may well end up having to accept some things that they do not like or agree with. When we leave decisions to others we have to accept that they will use their judgment and not ours, and that the conclusions they arrive at will be based on their values and assumptions. If we refuse to participate then we risk decisions being taken that do not concur with our worldview. This means it is possible for politicians to take decisions that do not necessarily meet with the approval of large parts of the public that they represent. In Britain, Parliament has outlawed the death penalty since the mid 1960s, despite there being an apparent majority in favour of it. Successive governments in the UK have both widened and deepened the links with the European Union despite this being generally unpopular and there being a clear majority of scepticism towards Europe in the country. More recently, governments across the developed world have used public money to bail out banks that behaved recklessly and irresponsibly. Again, this action is apparently in the face of public opposition. Politicians, who are elected, and need to seek re-election, are seemingly capable of ignoring large sections of public opinion with relative impunity and act counter to what their electorate might want them to do, especially during times of economic plenitude (sustainable or otherwise). We are even content to be bribed with our own money (or that of our children and grandchildren).

What complicates the matter is that the public are not unaware of this distance between their own views and those of their elected representatives. This becomes all too apparent with the issue of immigration. There appear to be two completely different sets of views which operate: those of the general public, which is hostile to immigration, and that of conventional political discourse, which only allows for the issue to be discussed in a particular manner, with serious consequences if it is breached.

There is certainly a degree of resentment felt by many that politicians do not represent the country when it comes to immigration. There is a distance between the common-sense view and that of the political elites. During the 2010 General Election immigration was virtually ignored by the politicians, but journalists and opinion polls continually reported that immigration was one of the electorate's main concerns. However, it is also true that what would most harm a politician's career is not support for immigration but its opposite. If a politician were to make the sort of comment that one can hear most days in the bus queue or in a shop their career would be finished, as was the case with a Conservative Parliamentary candidate who argued in 2007 that 'Enoch Powell was right' and was promptly forced to resign as a candidate.[7] So it would appear that not only did Powell ruin his own career through his comments on race, but nearly forty years later they are still too strong to support. What was particularly interesting was that those forcing the candidate to resign did not need to present any evidence one way or the other, but merely to assert that such comments were totally unacceptable and the candidate was gone.

During the election campaign itself, Gordon Brown, the Labour leader and Prime Minister, was overheard referring to an elderly woman in Rochdale as a 'bigot' because she has mentioned her concern over the impact of immigration. This was considered to be a gaffe and that this would affect Labour's performance in the election. There was considerable debate that immigration was a concern and that the politicians were indeed out of touch with public opinion.[8] Yet it is difficult to argue that this issue really affected the

7 See http:/www.timesonline.co.uk/tol/news/politics/article2804407.ece (accessed 1 March 2011)

8 See http://news.scotsman.com/uk/General-Election-2010-Immigration-39a.6260800.jp (accessed 1 March 2011)

Labour Party in any major way. Indeed it managed to hold onto the Rochdale constituency where Brown made his gaffe. Immigration might be seen as a major concern, and politicians seen as out of touch, but it did not make or break the election campaign.

The question therefore is why does the majority, which apparently consistently opposes immigration, do so little about it? Why was the clamour of support for the Conservative candidate not so strong that he could save his career? Why was it possible for the leadership of the Conservative Party to act in a manner that seemed so out of touch with majority opinion? Why did the public not respond more severely towards Labour over Brown's gaffe?

My aim here is not to explore the rights and wrongs of immigration. This is clearly a complex and contested issue and one that raises strong feelings. Instead I wish to consider how it is possible that such a controversial issue can be treated so differently by the public and politicians, and, more particularly, how can this distinction be maintained.

It would be very easy to blame the politicians for ignoring the views of 'ordinary people' and for being out of touch. But these politicians need to be elected to do anything and so have to garner the support of the public. And the public seems to vote for parties and politicians who do not prevent immigration and who have given away power to the EU on border controls. Those parties that have based their politics on ending immigration have generally fared badly. The British National Party, as the main party calling for an end to immigration, has never been near to a major electoral breakthrough. They may get some representation on local councils and gain some success in European elections when the voting system allows, but they are not competitive with the major parties.

Of course, we might suggest that this situation is due to the peculiarities of the British first-past-the-post electoral system, which tends to marginalise minority parties and over-emphasises the electoral support of the larger parties. The difference with European elections is that they are undertaken with a form of proportional representation and so the minor parties might gain some purchase. However, this change in the voting system does not encourage the major parties to adopt a populist view on immigration. We also have to note that when the British electorate was given the opportunity to vote for a new electoral system in May 2011 they soundly rejected it.

So we have this apparent paradox: the general public are said to be opposed to immigration, yet it has not been curtailed. Indeed the Labour Party managed to be re-elected in both 2001 and 2005 even though its policy on immigration was considerably more liberal than its opponents and that of governments in the recent past. The Labour Government managed quite successfully to silence any debate on immigration, and certainly after 2001, the Conservative opposition seemed more than happy to help. And they got away with it: those who oppose immigration – the apparent majority – seemed impotent in the face of the politicians' refusal to engage.

But where does the impotence come from? Why is it there? There is not, or does not seem to be, any active or intentional conspiracy against the commonsense view. After all, this view on immigration has its supporters in the popular press. There are a number of possible explanations for this situation, which are not mutually exclusive. The first answer is that most of us, most of the time, accept the legitimate authority of government. We are law-abiding and do what the law tells us. Of course, there are exceptions and law-breaking is by no means rare. Yet we accept the institutions and traditions of government. Indeed, we might not actually be terribly aware of these institutions and traditions. They operate without our active consent, other than through elections, and do not require our active engagement. The constitution, the government and parliament all work in a particular manner, with no need for our direct input. They have an established authority and this is accepted, albeit implicitly and without any citizen necessarily needing to be aware of it.

A point allied to this is that the political traditions and established practices of a country, and the means of political discourse, all mitigate against active participation and dictate the nature of any protest. There are very few means to affect change or to influence things other than the mainstream channels. Systems such as those in the UK and US that encourage a small number of dominant parties limit the form of political engagement to that dictated by party managers and leaders.

Third, the nature of modern government tends to mean that decisions are relatively small and appear inconsequential. The decisions taken by politicians do not appear to be too far-reaching in each individual case. Changes are incremental and no one particular change alters what we perceive as being normal. Those who are badly affected by any decision remain a small minority and so can be readily ignored by the rest of us. In any case, there may be no consensus on the nature of the problem or the means of correcting it.

Fourth, there is no organisation to support these elements of public opinion. The priorities of most people are elsewhere, away from politics and current affairs and are focussed instead on more mundane and everyday issues. This, it seems to me, is the crucial point: we are busy living our lives and are more than happy to allow politicians and those sufficiently interested in politics to manage the affairs of state. Even though many may complain about politicians, and even think ill of them, most people are more than happy that there is someone taking the decisions. We would rather these decisions were taken by others rather than by ourselves. We do not want to take part: we neither have the time, the patience, or the expertise. We will support the party that we feel best serves our interest, even though there may be elements of that party's programme which we would not support. Many Labour voters do not support the party's position on immigration but continue to vote for it because of other parts of Labour's programme and because of its historical role. In the words of Labour MP Frank Field:

> One issue stands out from canvassing core Labour voters over more than four decades. Many of our supporters hold social views well to the right of the Conservative party and offer opinions on asylum that the British National Party tries to reflect. Yet they vote Labour, not just through habit, but because the party has convinced them it is on their side. The unspoken compact is that Labour voters let the elite peddle social policies that often appal them, in return for the economic protection a Labour government has historically delivered.[9]

9 *Sunday Times*, 17 October 2004.

But this lack of organisation also means that we tend to see ourselves as just one isolated voice amongst millions. When these voices come together and coalesce around an issue then it does become powerful, as proved by the Tea Party movement in the 2010 US midterm elections. But there is no natural tendency for this coalescence to occur. When we vote it is just as likely to end in the stalemate of European elections when, for example, it took over two months to form a viable government in the Netherlands after elections in the summer of 2010. There is no organising principle, no centre and no necessary fixative to ensure that apparently isolated individuals come together and find a common voice. In many cases not enough people come together at the right time, or perhaps the issues are never quite big enough and so it does not ever develop sufficiently. On occasions it flares up, like the fuel protests in the UK in 2000. But these may subside just as quickly. It is quite rare for an issue to develop to such an extent that it has a permanent impact.

In any case, even these so-called mass protests never involve anything approaching a majority of people. Some issues may claim the implicit support of millions but this will still not constitute a real majority. Most remain on the sidelines, perhaps watching with some interest but otherwise carrying on with their lives.

So there are a number of reasons why individuals might feel that politicians do not represent them, but remain impotent to change this situation. It is partly due to institutional and organisational issues, but it is also, and mostly, due to our attention being elsewhere. What this leaves us with is a sense of disquiet or disaffection, but one that seldom if ever rises above a murmur. We may complain about those who take decisions, but we have no inclination to take over the decision making for ourselves. We may feel that politicians and governments do no speak for us, but we do nothing to make them more accountable or even to tell them to act differently. These feelings will ebb and flow as issues dictate. The Tea Party movement is a clear example of this disquiet swelling into something significant and possibly long term. In the UK, the parliamentary expenses scandal in 2009 created a growing swell of disgust and outrage about how politicians behave, but it did not lead to any significant and long-term change. This latter example is perhaps more typical: an issue comes along that, for a time, brings people together, giving them something to focus upon, but which then dissipates and our everyday concerns crowd back in and our attention shifts.

I want to suggest that this disquiet is a form of reaction. It is rather different from that more intellectual and considered version discussed in the previous chapter. It remains unarticulated and has no focus or centre. Yet it is still a form of reaction. This, to return to Burke's metaphor, is the cattle grazing quietly in the field ignoring the chink of a few noisy grasshoppers. This is the relatively quiet part of the population that just gets on with its own affairs and does not listen to the noise of politics. They are not noticed: they make no discernible noise and so are not heard. Yet when roused they can be a considerable force and will trample over the tiny creatures creating the din.

But why should we see this disquiet as a form of reaction? Would it not make more sense simply to describe this as apathy or ignorance?

III

The first task, therefore, is to try to substantiate such a thing as commonsense reaction. I believe that we can suggest that there is a disquiet towards politics and politicians. It can be characterised by a number of statements, which, while not all being mutually compatible, provide us with a picture of the form it takes. All these statements, if they were ever to be articulated, would be personalised. They would not be stated in the abstract, but as things which 'I' or 'we' feel, and I shall state them accordingly without this necessarily suggesting any affinity with the views.

The first statement is that we are not listened to by those in authority. Instead we are ignored by the decision makers who simply follow their own interests. This is because we see that politicians and others who take decisions — who we will insist in referring to as 'them' — are different from us. They have distinctly different motives and interests, which lead them to take up positions that we find bewildering and cannot fathom. They seem to actively enjoy giving sovereignty away to Europe and to bail out foreigners while cutting back at home. We find the views of 'their' interests to be perverse and strange and divorced from the world in which we live.

But, second, we have no real expectation that politicians will be like us. We expect them to be different and act in their perverse ways. Thus we are not particularly surprised by their actions. We may be disappointed but that merely confirms our prejudices. We do not expect politicians to be any different from how they are, or to do anything different from what they currently do.

Third, we believe that while things could be doubtless better, they could also be a lot worse: life may not be exactly good but it is also 'not bad'. We tend to describe the world without excessive enthusiasm: we see things as 'not bad', or as 'fair to middling'. We express ourselves negatively rather than with a positive statement. We acknowledge that things are OK, all right, or perhaps we will admit that they could be better, we do not wish to claim that things are perfect or anywhere near to that state. We do not have any particular problem as such, but we are not prepared to overstate. We do not wish to embarrass ourselves by a show of enthusiasm; we do not wish to go too far. If we said that things were bad or excessively good we might be drawn to explain ourselves, to make some definitive statement on our condition when we would rather not be drawn.

But, fourthly, we also do not believe that we have to explain ourselves any further. We do not feel that we need to justify our actions and beliefs to others. There is little wrong with how we live, and if anyone complains about us the problem is therefore with them not us. We feel that we are best able to decide how we should live and do not need or welcome the advice of others. We consider it to be perfectly proper, natural even, to ignore those things that we do not like or feel to be unimportant, and we do not see it as acceptable for anyone to tell us otherwise. We do not believe we need to question or examine our actions and resent any attempt by others to force us to do so. We believe that we are right and have no need to put our views to the test unless we ourselves choose to do so.

But having said this, we expect other people to be just like us and we are not that often disappointed. We assume a commonality of interests and beliefs. We expect our view of the world to be mirrored by those around us and so make ready assumptions in our conversations about what we understand to be normal and acceptable.

Finally, even though things are 'not bad' and we see no need to question our positions, if asked we would probably state that we expect that things are more likely to get worse than to get better. We may not be able to cite any reasons for this other than our singular experience. We have become somewhat cynical and jaundiced about the motivations and competence of politicians and it matters little which particular group of politicians are currently taking the decisions.

There is no particular consistency between these statements, but this is not something to be surprised at. We do not live according to a set of worked-out principles or a manifesto of intent. We act and react because of circumstance and situation, and these include convention and custom. We face particular situations and all we have to hand is our experience and a commonsense understanding of the world. We do not have to articulate it because it is never put under concerted attack. Instead we merely react as and when the circumstances dictate. This is most certainly not an intellectual position, but one where we act out of habit and on the basis of a belief that it is a right and proper way in which to behave.

While there is no necessary consistency in these statements, we do not think of ourselves as being inconsistent and nor would we not appreciate being referred to as such. We do not think of ourselves as crude calculating machines, but as making normal responses like anyone else would. We do not see ourselves as flawed beings, but rather we assume ourselves to be just acting, reacting and responding with no great intent or purpose.

We do not seek to question the motives of others any more that we examine our own. We might see ourselves as acting normally but, for the most part, we do not see the actions of others with anything other than a benign indifference. However, it is precisely this indifference that allows others – and therefore ourselves, as it is, of course, mutual – to actively seek to fulfil their own ends relatively free from interference. We rely on the indifference of others and so our diffidence has a purpose. It ensures people keep their distance from others, and so no one imposes themselves upon us, and nor do we impose on them.

An essential part of this commonsense form of reaction is an acceptance of the world as it is. It means that we have come to terms with how things are, rather than assuming that they could be something else. We accept our place and do not hanker to be someone else or elsewhere. This is not because our lives are perfect, or that we are always happy and content with our lot, but rather it is simply because we appreciate that we cannot be anywhere else but where we currently are. We will have aspirations, and some of these will be misplaced and unachievable, but we can adjust without too much difficulty. We may have regrets and still harbour hopes for the future, but these are grounded in our current reality. We accept that there are limits and understand that these cannot easily be transcended.

Indeed it is this acceptance of our position that makes it a form of reaction. Being aware of our limits and the groundedness of our current position means that we will tend to favour the present over the future. We will accept that what we have now is not contingent or based on some false understanding or consciousness. We are not being oppressed by unseen hegemonic forces that seek to bend us to their will, and we are not hankering after some utopian future where we believe that the world can be fundamentally different from how it is now. We know that this is all there is, and find it absurd to be told otherwise.

What causes us to react is precisely when this sense of order is compromised or challenged. It is when the comfortable relation between us, the governed, and those we have placed above us to govern breaks down that our disquiet begins to show and perhaps turns to anger. We feel we can no longer carry on as before and that we can no longer trust those in government. In the terms we discussed earlier, our complacent sense of self is being challenged.

Commonsense reaction is the opposite of an engaged interest and activism in politics. It does not favour direct involvement and appears instead to maintain a happy disdain towards politics. This does not mean that politics is completely disregarded, but rather that it does not feature in any active way. We know that politicians are out there, and that they are doing things. But we do not accept that they are the same as us and that our interests coalesce. Politicians are people who do things for themselves and on the basis of their interests. We accept this and only become agitated when we see that their actions become too outrageous for us to ignore any longer. For the most part we are able to remain disengaged and to pursue our own interests and so keep any disquiet at bay. Our resistance to action may be quite strong – we have much better things to do – but there will come a time when we are roused, whether it is because of the size of the deficit or the corrupt actions of politicians.

This discussion would suggest that this form of reaction is not an organised entity as such. It is not something we could take out membership of and there is no consensus view or party line. No one sets out or adheres to any programme or plan. Commonsense reaction should be seen as a feeling or disposition. It is an attitude that we may have, which derives from a sense of stability, of traditions, habits and accepted patterns of behaviour, of belonging to a culture and a place, all of which are still maintained, but which may, from time to time, be perceived as being under threat. We have established ways of behaving and this, in turn, provides us with ways of responding to situations as and when they arise. These established ways condition how we act and allow us a degree of complacency. This might offset or sublimate any sense of upheaval or disaffection we have. It provides us with roots that bind us to a place and a culture, and also with ruts that provide us with established means of navigating ourselves towards others (King, 2005).

Commonsense reaction will therefore often remain inchoate, formless and without an apparent purpose or direction. It has no aim, no unified purpose to fulfil; it has no principles to adhere to. It exists as a static sense of mute hostility against an unresponsive elite. It takes the form of silent or quiet resentment, perhaps rising to mild irritation and concern. As we have suggested, it is a sense of disquiet: a feeling that 'all is not quite right in the world, but what can we do about it?'

Where it becomes manifest is in the casual conversations we have with others about the news: why, we ask, are we giving money to help bail out the Irish whilst trying to pay off our own deficit and having to borrow ourselves? Why is immigration still rising when there are no jobs or houses for those of us here already? Why are so few people sent to prison, and why do the victims of crime get picked on and not the perpetrators? These are part of the passing conversations we have with others, squeezed in between discussions of the *X Factor* contestants, the weather and the football scores. Each particular encounter is inconsequential and without any attempt at resolution. We do not seek to change anything by our conversation, and all we do is merely confirm each other's views. They have involved no real thought or commitment on our part, and the conversation may have actually contained nothing but clichés and second hand thoughts gained from the previous encounter we might have had. But this does not matter. Rather these encounters confirm our place in the world by passing on the commonsense view. The contact shows us that we fit in with others and that we are part of something bigger than ourselves. We find that there is an 'us' – a 'we' – that stands up against 'them', against those who take all the decisions and seek to make our lives as they are. Indeed these contacts help us to realise that 'they' do not make our lives. Instead we are making them by our very encounters with others. We are confirming and reconfirming how things are and we do this for others as we nod and accept what they tell us as part of ourselves, as part of the ongoing 'we'.

As a result of this contact with others we perhaps feel a bit better about ourselves. We have made contact with others and found that they agree with us. Perhaps we take some comfort in knowing that we are not alone in thinking as we do: there is some commonality. But this happens without anything changing and so we venture off to complete our daily chores, feeling a little lighter, a little freer, in that we are not alone. We might be cheered by the connection we have made with others and perhaps as a result feel less distressed by the state of the world. Our prejudices have been confirmed and so all is as it should be.

These inconsequential, but affirming, contacts are all very separate from politics. It is as if there is something going on apart from us, which we are commenting on. We know that this affects us: the decisions taken by government, parliament and by local councillors do matter to us; it is 'our' money they are using to bail out Ireland: it is being done by 'our' government on 'our' behalf. But we still see it as a case of 'us' and 'them'. We are not fully part of it. We have not been asked to subscribe to the collective 'we' that is sending money to Ireland: it does not come, as it were, from out of us. We do not feel party to these decisions and actions. They are not being taken by people who feel as we do, and the decisions do not really seem to be in our interests. The government (and it is always 'the government' because nothing ever changes in this regard – 'they are all the same whoever wins the election') seems to have its own agenda; the government seems to be following its own interests that are apart from us. Indeed, we might begin to feel that elected elites actually have a disdain for the views of the 'ordinary' person: as Gordon Brown showed after his encounter in Rochdale, politicians often do have contempt for those they purportedly serve.

But this disquiet does not lead us to revolt. Instead we merely mutter and moan. We might change who we will vote for at the next opportunity, but we might not even do this: we might be too ingrained in our habits. We might decide not to vote, so as not to encourage them, but we know this does not help: as the old anarchist slogan goes: 'the government always gets in'.

And, of course, in a very important sense, we are not really impotent. Our votes, when taken together, can make a difference. We can change things as the Tea Party movement in the US has shown. They have ensured that some candidates have been elected and others defeated, as well as helping to shift opinion away from the Democrats. So there are occasions when hitherto inarticulate voices can come together and cause change. This, however, is unpredictable and often only noticeable with hindsight. What matters is the political psychology of the moment. It is this that stops us acting or propels us into the fray. Jon Elster (1993) discusses this sense of political psychology and relates it to the idea of revolution. Why do some people risk almost certain defeat, torture and even death by being the first to revolt? Why do they seek to lead an uprising when they must know that failure is near certain? What makes them discount this risk and take up the challenge of toppling the establishment? But then at what point is a critical mass achieved that changes the stakes and allows many – the majority – to join without the great personal risk of the founders? How do we judge when this moment has occurred? What turns these otherwise apathetic, uninterested or frightened individuals into a community of interest ready to be led? It is easy to follow when we can hide in a crowd but how to get to the point of forming the crowd, how to bring it together out of the apathetic and the fearful?

What helps those who join first and seek to lead is a clear set of beliefs and a sense of certainty in their rectitude. They may also believe that they actually represent majority opinion. They see themselves as the advance guard that, by protesting, open the eyes of the majority and make change seem a reality. They may believe this even though they form an infinitesimally small minority, and sustain this by the certainty of their worldview: unlike others, they have seen the 'truth', and so have something to sustain them. We saw this attitude in 2010 with the violent protests against raising student tuition fees in the UK. A small number of the community marched in London, and a tiny part of these rioted and committed acts of violence and did so in the name of 'the people', in the apparent belief that they were representing the majority, who may, for the time being, remain silent, but who are certainly on their side. Perhaps they believe that the majority needs to be educated and made aware of their interests – this is why they actively challenge authority to show its true nature – but they still believe they act for the broad mass. A similar point could be made regarding the secular liberals at the vanguard of the 'Arab spring'. After the votes have been counted the Tahrir Square radicals appear very different from the conservative Islamic majority of their countrymen.

These protestors, of course, are no more representative than any other group of random individuals (perhaps less so precisely because of their interest in politics and the extreme lengths they go to persuade others of their rectitude). The student fees riots and demonstrations took place only six months after an election in which twenty million people voted and left us with a government that represents 60% of that vote. What allows the protestors to act as if they represent the majority is that most of us remain quiet: it simply would not occur to us to make any claims to represent anyone but ourselves, or to believe that we could act and speak on anyone's behalf. We have our contacts with others, be it at work, through family, or in our neighbourhood. We readily accept that all other people are the same as we are, in the sense of having rights and responsibilities – they are as human as us. However, in practical terms, we see the world as 'us' and 'them', as a few significant people and then the rest. Only a very few people stand out for each of us. This is not the result of any animosity or ill feeling toward others, and nor is it rooted in resentment or aggression. It is merely a natural sense of separation that allows us to pursue our own ends without undue coercion from others. This is, of course, a mutual state: we ignore those who are ignoring us. Each individual might, in a certain sense, be seen as typical, but there is no claim here to represent or speak on behalf of others. There is no particular presumption here about living a life on behalf of anything or anyone else apart from ourselves.

It would be a mistake to see this as in anyway selfish, although it is quite naturally self-interested. We are not being greedy and seeking to take what is not ours. We are not abusing others or using them for our benefit. We are not necessarily even maximising anything. We are merely doing what we think is best for ourselves and our own, and letting others do likewise.

It is only through this benign indifference of others that we can act as we wish to. We are left alone to pursue our own ends, and this is because these others are busy pursuing their own ends too. There is nothing in this but a normal sense of propriety and self-interest, with people focusing on what matters and interests them.

We might describe this indifference to others as a form of practical autonomy, as the quiet enjoyment of our lives and the consequences that flow from our own actions. It too remains inchoate and unarticulated. If we were to ask others to define this sense of autonomy – to articulate what it is and what it means to them – we might face confusion and even some hostility for our impertinence. It is by no means clear what it is other than our daily routines practised amidst others, and there is no way often to put this into words. Of course, likely responses to our questioning, such as 'Mind your on business!' and 'What do you want to know for?' are themselves instructive. They detail the very self-possession and self-interest at the root of our sense of self.

What our questions do is to challenge the benign and non-threatening self-centredness at the heart of our social actions. Accordingly, when challenged and seemingly made to articulate this sense of self, we might become prickly and react badly to our interrogator.

So we might suggest that the lack of articulation and unfocussed nature of commonsense reaction is crucial to its viability. To focus on it, to put it under too close a scrutiny, would be to damage it and stop it operating. It works through informal convention and by limiting the engagement we have with others. Without this, by becoming too conspicuous, we might see how tenuous our sense of self actually is and how open we are to abuse. Like most forms of psychology, it operates by being unnoticed and uncommented on.

This lack of articulation should not, however, detract from the force and seriousness of our need for distance. It is a necessary form of relationship and needs to remain unformed. Without it we would have no autonomy, no freedom to act. Many of our actions are dependent on the natural and conventional constraint of others, on their normal refusal to interfere, their natural, normal and quite expected indifference to us. So our actions in this sense do not depend upon articulated principles but on unspoken conventions derived out of the reiterated actions of others and ourselves. It is not what we do, but what we do not do to others that matter. It is our restraint, and the conventions that bind these in, that perpetuate our sense of self. This might suggest that our rights, our autonomy, are quite precarious, depending as they do on convention rather than principle. Yet we have merely to compare societies based on conventions, be they traditional societies or modern liberal democracies, with those societies based on abstract principles such as the former Soviet bloc, to realise the strength of convention as an organising principle. Once the state collapsed in Russia and Romania they was no residual solidarity, but rather the opposite. There was nothing to replace the state's artificially enforced solidarity and community: state action had driven out autonomous actions and created a passivity that could not response to the real exigencies of communal life.

Commonsense reaction cannot be described as an elitist position, but then nor can it be termed as inclusivist, at least not in the manner that the word is now used. We do not seek to include all others, but rather to admit that there is a general disposition or attitude that seeks to resist changes imposed upon us from outside. This does not mean solidarity in any political sense, but a quiet sense of being all together, 'us' against 'them'. In most cases we do not discuss our attitudes, but they will rather come out as and when circumstances dictate. We respond to issues and then might come together with others, to share our views, to support the statement of others, or to show our disaffection. But we do not take this as being demonstrative of some deeper form of unity or bond between us.

Indeed instead of inclusivity, commonsense reaction might be more likely to carry with it a sense of exclusion, a feeling of being on the outside. We sense that the world is no longer the one we had become familiar with. We fail to understand it anymore, and seem to find it difficult to follow what is happening. We do not feel that our opinions are sought by those in power: we are simply not consulted about the big decisions which affect us and instead they are taken despite us. The world passes us by and this is the cause of our disaffection.

But, of course, we make no attempt to get involved ourselves, and so there is a contradiction again. This, however, can be explained quite simply: even though we feel excluded, we still feel that we are in the mainstream. We consider that we are part of the majority, and that we hold the 'normal' views and are not out on a limb. It is the politicians and commentators who are the eccentrics who hold the outlandish views that are out of step with how real people think. As a result, we feel usurped by an elitist and unrepresentative minority represented by politicians and the media.[10] Some people might go so far as to suggest that there is some sort of conspiracy that seeks to exclude us,

---

10 Peter Oborne has estimated the size of the modern (and homogeneous) UK political-media class to approximate 5,000 souls (Oborne, 2007). By contrast Anthony Sampson's 1960's 'establishment' was larger and considerably more diverse, there being 'not a single Establishment, but a ring of Establishments. The friction and balances between the different circles are the supreme safeguard of democracy' (Sampson, 1962, p. 624).

which refuses to take us seriously, or to listen to our concerns and instead contemptuously ignores us. We might consider that there is a 'metropolitan elite' that rules despite us, ignoring our concerns and focusing on a set of issues inimical to our interests. This will not necessarily take a party-political form, in that we do not distinguish between left and right, or between liberals and conservatives. As far as the Tea Party movement was concerned, the Republican Party in the US appeared as out of touch as the Democrats over issues like the deficit. Many Republican candidates found themselves targeted as 'Rinos' – Republican in name only – and were opposed in the 2010 Congressional elections. Indeed several were replaced by candidates with views more amenable to the aims of the Tea Party movement. Likewise, despite being in opposition, Conservative MPs in the UK found they were as tainted as Labour ones by the scandal over parliamentary expenses in 2009. The feelings were against all those in politics and because they were 'all the same'.

What commonsense reaction does reject is the accepted view of the political elite. It does not accept the apparently sophisticated view of politicians that the issues are too complex to be understood by the majority, and therefore that promises cannot always be kept, or that compromise is necessary even when this had not made clear in advance. Instead it takes the simple view that politicians should mean what they say and that their actions should bear some relation to those statements. They do not accept that moving away from this simple view is in any way sophisticated or more informed. It merely shows that politicians are a different form of life than normal people.

This position can be quite readily described as a rather tabloid view of the world. It seems to accept the knee jerk view of the popular red top newspapers, who, it is accused, seek to pander to prejudice in order to maintain their sales figures. Instead of informing their readers these newspapers provide an unthinking, simplistic and unreflective view. Indeed, in the UK one can frequently hear the words *The Daily Mail* used to characterise this particular view. In stating these words the speaker assumes certain things that apparently need no further qualification: merely to say *The Daily Mail* is enough, and no more discussion is necessary.

The particular position is damned and the person expressing it expelled from right-thinking company. And what is particularly appalling to all right-thinking people is that *The Daily Mail* is the second most widely-read, and perhaps has the greatest influence, of any newspaper in the country.

The Daily Mail is indeed a very popular newspaper, yet it often seems to be representing those it sees as disenfranchised, unheard and powerless. The newspaper identifies with those it considers are not being listened to or taken seriously. It seeks to represent those who are outside the establishment and who feel marginalised by it. But considering the readership of *The Daily Mail* this cannot really be the case as it is taken by governments of both left and right as a weather vane of public opinion. This might suggest that this sense of powerlessness and disenfranchisement is false and merely a marketing ploy. Is it an act on the part of journalists to garner support by creating and maintaining a sense of resentment? But if it is false how has it come about and why does it persist? Why should a newspaper that is so widely read seek to portray its readers as having no importance?

It is unlikely to be due to ignorance, in that the newspaper is clearly capable of attracting a good share of the market. A more plausible reason is that this newspaper, along with a number of others, has sought to tap into the sense of disaffection we have been describing. It is a part of the commonsense reaction I have suggested exists. The readership of these newspapers are not part of the decision-making elite, and in terms of outlook, education and locale they are very different from the idea of the affluent metropolitan elite who are taken to be running the country, whether it be typified by Tony Blair or David Cameron. What we have then is a part of the media that is capable of associating with commonsense reaction. Working in this media are a number of what can be called public intellectuals, such as James Delingpole, Simon Heffer, Douglas Murray, Peter Oborne and Melanie Philips, who operate outside of the mainstream intellectual elite, and instead represent this more commonsensical view of the world. These intellectuals do not accept the received views of the BBC and the left-of-centre media, but speak for what they see as a disenfranchised majority.

Now there is another contradiction here: the most popular and most widely-read newspapers are those that represent that opinion which runs counter to the establishment. However, what should be recognised here is the common perception rather than the actuality of the situation. And what this shows is that there is a considerable body of opinion that considers itself to be outside the mainstream. Indeed, it might be the case that this view is actually the majority. But, precisely because it considers itself disenfranchised and so withdraws from any active engagement in politics, it remains relatively impotent and the establishment continues on.

But this sense of being on the outside allows the idea that commonsense reaction is based on ignorance to persist. It is all too easy for those with more defined and articulated principles to portray this commonsense view as ignorant and unenlightened. It can be written off as the view of an under-educated mass, who are too full of prejudices to be listened to or respected. They cannot, and should not, be taken seriously by those who are educated and capable of having and making an opinion.

This is another example of political psychology, where a minority take their certainty as representing something beyond themselves. But we should not see commonsense reaction as especially ignorant. It rather does not appreciate or particularly understand the views of the minority who consider themselves opinion-formers. These two groups simply do not see the world in the same manner. Instead of basing their ideas on rational principles, reactionaries ground their beliefs in lived experiences. They have little time for abstractions, and their ideas are not addressed on the basis of preconceived principles. Instead issues are reacted to on a piecemeal basis. So, we can actually say that many progressives will tend to come to an issue with a prejudged perspective[11] (we should note here, the old meaning

[11] The early-modern republican theorist James Harrington argued that elites were primarily distinguished by their ability to articulate interests, and for this reason awarded them policy-proposal rights in his influential constitutional blueprint, *The Commonwealth of Oceana* (1656). Judgement, however was reserved exclusively for randomly-selected members of the general citizenry.

of the word 'prejudice') based on habit, and which they seek to apply to any given set of circumstances.

What can make commonsense reaction appear to be ignorant is that, precisely because it is a reaction, the opinions expressed may appear to be derivate and clichéd. There is no sophistication, complexity or nuance in the arguments expressed, merely a common response that might not be capable of a full justification beyond a few stock phrases. But the very essence of reaction is its lack of originality. Originality is looked at with suspicion: it comes from an unknown place. How do we know what the new idea is based on, how can we trust it, and how do we gauge what effect it will have? The derived nature of commonsense ideas is what makes them so useful. But, in any case, the supposedly enlightened view can be seen as merely consisting of a different set of clichés. This is what is meant by 'political correctness', an approved means of responding based on preconceived notions linked to a prevailing ideology, such that arguments can only be acceptable if expressed in a particular manner.

What does not help commonsense reaction is that it has no independent means of generating arguments. Instead they spread and catch on like an infection, with no central organising point and not obvious lines of communication. We might say that people 'catch' a particular idea, and 'infect' others through contact. The ideas are not learned as such, and nor can there be a formal means of education. If it were, it would cease to be common sense and become something more formal. This might suggest that it is irrational, and there is indeed something in this. But the entire point of reaction is to shift with circumstance, and if these change then it would be entirely rational to alter one's position accordingly. Indeed, to do anything else would be perverse. As J.M. Keynes put it, 'When the facts change, I change my mind. What do you do, sir?'

Critics of commonsense reaction might wish to locate it in political terms, and see it as conservative. This might not be seen as problematic to some who hold this view, but for others the very idea of being associated with a political party would cause them difficulties. They see themselves as being anti-political, and against all forms of politics. For them, all politicians are the same and so it does not matter what label they carry. However, like conservatism, commonsense reaction is dispositional in nature. It is based on a set of attitudes rather than rational principles and ideas. This may mean a natural affinity with more conservative causes, as is certainly the case with the Tea Party movement in the US. However, once it becomes too overtly political there is the danger of it being adopted into the mainstream and so becoming a formal political entity.

But it does not especially matter if it is conservative or not, or how it develops into activism. What we are describing here is a sense of dissatisfaction with the world as it is, which will tend to remain latent and may not go beyond the occasional murmur. However, it can catch fire and turn into something more substantial. It may not be possible to predict when or how this might happen. In all probability it will remain rare and unpredictable. The reaction will normally be at a low level, and be contained below the surface. It will become manifest only in small asides, quips and comments, in apparently throwaway remarks when people come together by chance. But when it does catch fire it will do so in a manner that could not have been forecast in advance and which may not be containable. It will develop its own momentum and on its own terms. It may grow into something formal and permanent. It may take over existing institutions and movements. But then it may quickly die away and be forgotten, leaving behind little of consequence.

IV

What has given an added life to this commonsense notion of reaction is the recession that occurred after the financial crisis of 2007-8. Not only did this create high levels of distrust towards politicians and other elites, it also brought to the fore commonsense notions of fairness and responsibility. In particular, it altered the manner in which fairness is described and discussed. The left has tended to see fairness in terms of inequality and the difference between rich and poor. The Labour Government in the UK, particularly under the influence of Gordon Brown, followed this description of fairness and sought to create a fairer society through redistribution. However, as a result of the recession the debate on fairness has shifted more towards a focus on what outcomes individuals deserve on the basis of their actions. Fairness has come to be seen more in terms of desert and reciprocity rather than equality. One example of this has been a long debate in the UK and the US over the remuneration of bankers and whether they deserve the right to their large salaries in the light of their involvement in the financial crisis.

A key concept in discussing fairness is that of proportionality. So, for example, how much do the wealthy pay in taxes, and is this acceptable relative to what the poorest have to pay. If one earns more then one should pay more, and hence tax systems operate on the basis of the general acceptance of progressive taxation. What matters, in terms of fairness, are the shares that each part of society pays, and this should be relative to their income.

Yet we can see proportionality in a rather different manner, in terms of reciprocity and desert. What matters here is whether one gets out what one pays in; whether contributions and receipts are reasonable and properly balanced across all parts of the community; and whether the distribution of burdens and benefits is fair in terms of what each person has or has not done.

We can see fairness as being innate, in that children will tend to have a natural sense of what is fair and unfair in terms of how they are treated and relate to others. They do not seem to need to be told this or learn it. It is rather part of their ordinary sense of self. This doubtless is affected by custom and education, but we can say that unfairness has to be learnt. We see it as fair that we get equal shares of pie and arbitrary if we do not. We believe that there should be some proper system for allocating finite resources that applies equally to all unless there is a good reason for it not to. Hence we see the need to queue for things, and to take our turn. But we will also accept that others take precedence when it is clearly shown that they have a greater objective need such as serious illness or homelessness. Likewise, we are prepared to make sacrifices or to incur costs, but only so long as others do as well, and that the reasons for undertaking those burdens are justified. Accordingly, we will feel aggrieved if others are seen to be benefitting unreasonably at our expense. Similarly it is not uncommon to hear someone claim that they would willingly pay more tax to fund, say, healthcare or education. But what they tend to mean here is that they are prepared to pay more *so long* as everyone else does along with them. They want to raise taxes for all not just to pay more themselves. Otherwise they could simply send a cheque to their local hospital or school.

A problem can arise when different senses of fairness come clash. New Labour appeared to see fairness as a matter of how much government spent on certain groups and on the measurement of certain outcomes for these groups compared to others higher up the income scale. Getting more equality between groups in terms of spending and income was therefore seen as achieving fairness. However, this took no regard of a more commonsense view of fairness, which was concerned with what was reasonable and proper for people to receive in terms of the contributions that they had made. Accordingly, households receiving over a £1000 per week in Housing Benefit, without having to do anything to earn this other than prove their 'need', was seen as being grossly unfair by those having to pay for this benefit through their taxes, but who could not afford similar-quality housing granted to those apparently in 'need'. This form of provision was consequently very unpopular and became hard to justify in a period of fiscal retrenchment. Accordingly, in 2010 when the Cameron government proposed to cap Housing Benefit to £400 per week this was widely approved of, even as it was seen as controversial by opposition politicians and some parts of the media. It created a short-term political reaction but once it became clear that the proposals were generally popular with the public, and seen by them as fair, the opposition in Parliament to the proposals diminished markedly. Indeed there was still a degree of bemusement that households would still be able to claim a total of £21,000 a year in housing benefit, it having been calculated that a household would need a salary of around £70,000 to comfortably afford to fund annual mortgage payments of this size.

This form of welfare provision seemed to breach a commonsense notion of fairness based on proportionality and reciprocity. Of course, the situation has been made worse by the effects of the recession, which has hardened attitudes and made the general public less tolerant of what were now seen as excesses. They may have been tolerated before, although the scale of payment was not then so widely known. It was the recession, and the decision to cut spending as a result, that sparked the resentment and created the support for reform. But importantly it needed a government prepared to consider reform: the situation of excessive payments existed before 2010, but was ignored by politicians and the public. It took politicians to raise and develop the issue, and only then did the public sense of resentment at this unfairness became manifest. This, in turn bolstered the policy.

This suggests two issues pertinent to the discussion on commonsense reaction. The first is that, unlike the more intellectual form of reaction, the commonsense version needs a spark in order to turn it from a murmur to something more active. It needs something to generate it and give it form. Second, the issue of housing benefit shows that while this form of reaction is often latent, once it does become active it can quickly find a voice and a set of arguments to articulate. Once there is an issue to focus on, there is no lack of argumentation to support it, and these arguments might have a spontaneity and naturalness that matches that of the movement itself. Again, the Tea Party movement provides an example, with the ready use of the traditional American symbols of liberty and individual freedom coming quickly to the fore (O'Hara, 2010).

V

I have suggested that the period after 2008 has been one of increased disquiet. The financial crisis and the recession have added to the cut and thrust of politics and heightened the sense of resentment felt by many. We do not trust politicians and we now look differently on government and all its doings. This may well be temporary and we may quickly slip back to a more comfortable position. Once the debts are repaid and the budget is balanced – assuming they ever are – then we might return back to our more complacent state. As with most things, only time will tell. However, the fact that the levels of resentment will differ according to time and place is an important one.

But we also need to appreciate that even where there is a high level of resentment, this does not often amount to open revolt. Extreme measures are indeed very rare in a civilised democracy, which has well-established means for creating and for tempering change. We expect politicians and governments to act on our behalf and our reaction is based on our assessment of how well they have done this. What we will see therefore are different degrees of resentment and not revolution or fundamental change. As we have seen, even those such as Sarah Palin who called in 2010 for a 'revolution' in response to Barack Obama's policies was really just calling for the 'right' sort of Republicans to be elected. Within the narrow parameters of civilised political discourse, reaction is not really that far from the centre.

Of course, it might be that things do get out of hand, and so we need to consider the relationship between commonsense and violent reaction. In particular, is it possible that resentment might lead to revolution? Is it possible for commonsense reaction to turn into something that is violently out of control?

I would argue that, while it is never impossible for revolutions to occur, there is a fundamental block on the development of commonsense reaction into anything more serious than a shift in voting behaviour. This is because the very notion of common sense I have identified here, which is formed out a stable sense of self, is a function of a working democracy. Indeed, we might see the murmurings I have considered as the froth on the surface of democracy. This sense of disquiet is nothing but a product of the ebb and flow of civilised political debate. Violent revolution and political change, as we saw in North Africa in 2011, is more likely to be the result of autocracy and where a sense of overriding purpose and the belief in the rectitude of certain ideals leads to the suppression of dissent. This leaves no means for disquiet to surface and dissipate and so it in time may turn into something more solid.

Of course, as we saw in the previous chapter, counter-revolution is more typical of reaction than revolution itself. Reactionaries such as Joseph de Maistre (1850, 1974) eschew revolution but see the need for its opposite, for putting things back to how they once were, whether it be throne and altar, as in de Maistre's case, or restoring the original view of the US Constitution, as the Tea Party movement have called for (O'Hara, 2010). Counter-revolution is based on the premise that things can be returned to how they once were. It is therefore about change, albeit a backwards one. But commonsense reaction wants little of this sort of action. It does not see a return to past times as either tenable or necessarily desirable. There is much in how we live now that we wish to preserve, and this will include the creature comforts of a modern life. Where we are now is, by and large, pleasant. Of course, things could be better and there are things that annoy us and cause us some resentment. But 'now' is what we are used to and what we accept: it is simply how things are. The level of resentment we have is generally low level, and can be kept that way. It tends to increase only when our sense of complacency – our sense of how the world is – is challenged. In these cases we find we cannot ignore certain issues and we accordingly might make our discontent known.

So it is part of the very common sense we have been describing to see that even though many things are wrong with the world, for the most part we can get on with our lives and we need not consider extreme measures. Life is most assuredly not perfect, but neither is it terrible: there are parts of the world around us that we find hard to accept and do not like, but by and large things are not really that bad. We can live with things as they are, and so long as we can moan and show our feelings – that we have a safety valve – then we are happy to maintain things as they are.

VI

In this chapter and the previous one we have discussed two distinct forms of reaction: one that is intellectual and reasoned, and one that is inchoate and based on common sense. We have suggested that the latter form is not elitist, but is content with much of the world as it is. The intellectual reactionary, however, is overtly elitist, whether it is with regard to politics or to culture. In politics the aim of these reactionaries, we might suggest, is to stir up the quiet ones, to make politics come alive and appear important to them. They may see their role as tapping onto the commonsense views of their fellows to spread the doubt and suspicion they see as crucial to undermining progress. However, there may be no real sense of commonality, particularly with regard to mass involvement in politics, which many reactionaries would take as at best unfortunate.

A further elitist form of reaction is that which seeks to preserve a threatened cultural inheritance. This form of reactionary wishes for a return to a now lost or dying culture based on traditional forms of language, literature, art and music, as well as old forms of dress, values and propriety. These reactionaries are not separated from politics, but rather see politics often in cultural terms, as concerns over identity, religion and values as expressed in art, music and literature. This is the form of reaction we see described in the works of Russell Kirk (1986) and Roger Scruton (2001, 2007, 2009). Scruton argues for the preservation of long-standing cultural practices such as hunting with hounds, and against what he terms the culture of repudiation that leads to the denial of Western culture by the very people who have benefited from its highest levels of education. Scruton is critical of the effects of postmodernism and relativism as examples of this repudiation. Instead he argues for universal aesthetic values and discrimination between good and bad art, and between high and low culture. According to him, we can define something as beautiful and it is worthwhile for us to do so.

In some ways this cultural reaction might appear at odds with quiet reaction. It is, as we have suggested, avowedly elitist, being based on a long and difficult accumulation of knowledge and sensibility. But like all reaction the starting point here is the acceptance of the world as it is and not how utopians might seek to create it. Neither form of reaction wishes to repudiate the world as it has been formed. Whether we see this in terms of a cultural inheritance or in more quotidian terms is not as important as the shared acceptance of things as they are.

All the forms of reaction we have considered have broadly the same targets: the idea of progress. Reactionaries wish to preserve things, whether a culture, certain political institutions, or simply the life we are comfortable with. Those institutions and ways of life that are established and have stood the test of time need to be preserved. Common-sense reaction may involve little in the way of overt activity, while other reactionaries might be more active in their attempts to preserve things. But just as those wedded to common sense prove the utility of their lives by getting on with them, so elitists seek to preserve by showing the utility of the cultural items and institutions they hold dear. There are differences between forms of reaction, but this does not create problems of definition. Indeed we can question what part rigour and consistency matter in reaction, other than a consistent resistance to change and the call of progress. What matters is the 'being against' of reaction. What we need to do now, therefore, is to examine in more detail what they are against and what it might mean.

Chapter Four

Antimodern

I

Reactionaries see that something is wrong. The problem is what is to be done about it? Can the clock be turned back, or is it always a vain effort to stop progress and change? Can we ever return to a former age, when things were simpler and we seemed to be in control, and if not, is not reaction always doomed to fail? From our discussion thus far we would seem to suggest that this is the case: change continues and we can expect no other. We cannot hold out against it, and it seems futile to even try. So if change is permanent and the call for progress will never end what is the point of reaction? Why do we not just bow to the inevitable and accept our lot? Why cannot we come to terms with progress?

We have partially answered these questions already: it is precisely because of the inevitability of progress that reaction remains needed. As long as the call for progress is heeded, and mistakes and disasters occur as a result – which they will with the same grim inevitability as the call for progress itself – there will be the need for some to argue against it and try to put a brake on the speed of change. Reaction, we might suggest, remains worthwhile if it slows down attempts at progress and so lessens the prospect of disaster. If there is a way to make utopians stop and think and then to justify what they are doing there is some point to reaction. If it means that politicians have to show greater caution in their claims and their action, then it will be worth it.

But the existence of reaction does not simply rest on a question of success or failure. It is also a matter of belief: reactionaries think in certain ways and believe in certain things. Accordingly, we would expect them to say so, even if they fail to change anything. Would we expect the Labour Party to disband after its failure to stay in office in 2010, or the Republicans simply to go home when they lost the White House in 2008? Indeed, most political ideas end in failure, and reaction has as poor a track record as progress in this regard.

So it is not a matter of success or failure for those who believe in ideas. Of course, we hope, or even expect, our ideas to come to fruition, but we are more than content to put this off a little further into the future. In the meantime we have much to do: we have arguments to win and ideas to promote. Reactionaries have much to occupy them.

But what are they reacting to? Can we provide some sense of what it is that reaction, in its various guises, objects to? The argument that reaction has is with what we might refer to as *modernity*. This, as we shall see, is the notion that regards progress and change above all other things. It is the idea that progress is an end in itself and that a society or a culture should always be seeking to move forwards, accepting the new and rejecting outdated and redundant practices, institutions and habits.

The role of the reactionary, therefore, is to highlight the problems with modernity, arguing against those who insist on progress and change, and to point out the fallacies, fantasies and the hubris of utopians. It is to show that much of what passes for progress is unasked for and unwanted, and that the changes that result are unpredictable and often unforeseen. The role of the reactionary is to make the progressive think and slow down, ideally to a complete stop.

This raises an immediate question: can there be an alternative to modernism? This is a question that operates on two levels. First, if we see the modern as merely what is 'now', then clearly there cannot be any alternative: the modern is always where we are now, it being the latest form of our culture, that which is a progression from what came before. For most of us, most of the time, modernity is criticised only in its specifics rather than in general terms. We might complain about specific issues with modern society that annoy or distract us. This is indeed the case with commonsense reaction, which is not stated as a set of principles, but as particular complaints. And this suggests that there is much about the modern world – what is here now – that we will accept, enjoy and take for granted, and even insist upon. It is often not modernity as such that is the problem, rather particular aspects of the modern world.

But there is a problem with this view of modernity. Merely to see the modern as what is current would mean that the Taleban and Hamas are modern, as well as the Iranian theocracy. Yet these all reject what are seen as important elements of the modern world such as democracy, gender rights and freedom of expression. More particularly, there is little in common with the Taleban and Western democracies other than that they both currently exist and have some impact on the world around them. So, merely to use the term as a simple description of the present ensures that it becomes meaningless.

Modernity, we might feel, should mean more than this, and indeed it can be seen in more formal terms. More articulate reactionaries, such as Burke, de Maistre and Scruton, point to principles, and offer a comprehensive critique of modernity based on something more than dislike of specifics. Accordingly, the second way in which we can describe modernity is *those beliefs and actions that insist on the pursuit of progress and human perfectibility based on the application of reason*. It is this form that we shall concentrate on here. We wish to see modernity as meaning more than just the present: it is not merely intended to refer to the most advanced but to the very possibility that we can, and should, advance.

What reaction seeks to present then is a coherent antimodernism, and it this that I wish to explore here. We have considered what reaction is and how it might become manifested formally and in commonsense terms. What we now seek to do is to consider just what it opposes, what it is against, and what this might mean for the coherence of reaction itself. What I wish to explore is whether we can ever really be antimodern: can we ever get out of the modern, and what would it mean to try?

This does not mean that we seek to live outside of society. For most of us, who have commitments and our comforts to maintain, we would not find this in any way possible. But to be antimodern is not to suggest we reject society, even if it is properly defined as 'modern'. Instead it is where we see the idea of the modern as an attitude or view of the world rather than a specific time or place. It is the attitude of looking forwards and accepting progress as simply how the world is. It is where we place a premium on scientific rationality and administrative efficiency.

These are things that we can be against because they are ever present in our world. So we can be against the ideas of progress and efficiency where they disrupt the patterns of our lives. We can choose to look backwards and point to that which has been rejected and lost in the rush to change. We can treasure our past, our traditions and seek to defend them, arguing against those who would destroy them in favour of the hypothetical.

II

The starting point for our discussion on the antimodern is the Enlightenment, or rather what rose to oppose it. This movement, made up of French conservatives and reactionaries and German romantics has become known as the Counter-Enlightenment, a term coined by Isaiah Berlin (1997). The Counter-Enlightenment came to oppose the notions of progress, rationalism and sceptical enquiry that have formed the basis for much of modern thought. As Anthony O'Hear (1999) has stated, the differences between the Enlightenment and the Counter-Enlightenment are readily apparent:

> If the Enlightenment stressed reason, the Counter-Enlightenment stressed feeling. If the Enlightenment stressed science and modern civilisation, the Counter-Enlightenment stressed nature and the primitive life. It looked within, into our hearts, where the Enlightenment sought objectivity. Further, the Counter-Enlightenment emphasised the diversity of human society, and questioned the very notion of progress that saw modern societies as better than ancient of primitive ones.
>
> Human nature was not universal, it was particular and historical: different peoples had their own cultures and norms, and they could not be compared or judged prejudicially — from the point of one society or the other. And where the Enlightenment sought to found social institutions on human reason and human choices, the Counter-Enlightenment looked for religious foundations for society and morality. Finally, where the Enlightenment would submit all old beliefs to the test by contemporary scientific reason, the Counter-Enlightenment saw virtue in habits and beliefs just because they were old, because

> they had stood the test of time, because they embodied ancient and not necessarily immediately discernible wisdom. (p. 27)

We might summarise this distinction by stating that the Enlightenment sought to question all traditions, habits and institutions on the basis of a universal idea of reason, whereas the Counter-Enlightenment sought solace in the particular and the established and did so precisely because they were so specific and entrenched. Instead of looking where we want, or ought, to be, the Counter-Enlightenment sought to stress the utility of being just where we already are.

Berlin (1997) argues that 'one of the most interesting and influential' (p. 20) thinkers of the Counter-Enlightenment was Joseph de Maistre, a thinker we have consistently referred to as one of the mainstays of reactionary thought. De Maistre provided a critique of the modern, including the preference for the scientific method and rationalism over intuition and providence (de Maistre, 1996, 1998). Instead of the optimistic Enlightenment view of humanity as rational and capable of good, he put forward an understanding of humanity as by nature violent and aggressive. We do not come together naturally to co-operate and live peacefully, but rather we need discipline and order in our lives directed from above. Instead of maximising autonomy and freedom, the state needs to be the focus of authority and this should be absolute. There can be no compromise with democracy or the will of the people. This is a betrayal of the providential role of the state as the absolute determinant of the social order. In his *St Petersburg Dialogues* (de Maistre, 1993) he considers the role of the executioner as the symbol of this absolute sense of order. The executioner may be a figure treated with disgust and repugnance, but according to de Maistre, it is he who ensures the order of the whole.

De Maistre (1850) was a critic of what he saw as the burgeoning atheism of the post-Enlightenment period, with its denigration of the place of the church and papal authority. He sought to justify placing spiritual authority over the temporal. He argued that all societies have a religious basis to them that predates any form of temporal governance. All this can be seen as a justification for sustaining, and where necessary restoring, what is long established and traditional over what is new.

As Berlin (1997) argues, this can be taken as an extreme position, and we need not accept all or any of it. De Maistre was writing from within the specific milieu of the Enlightenment itself. He was not looking back with the benefit of 200 years of history, but from a position that saw the Enlightenment project as incomplete, and so as an active threat. In our day we face different threats and have different concerns. The battles of de Maistre's time have been lost and won and we are faced with that legacy. In other words, we have to react differently.

But we can still learn much from the attitude to change taken by de Maistre, by how he sought to contest the heady optimism of an Enlightenment that soon led to terror and violence. As Alain de Benoist (1993) has stated, we cannot know how figures such as de Maistre would respond in today's situation. But their perspective, de Benoist speculates, remains relevant in a world in which faith in progress is crumbling. We are now all too aware of the consequences and complexities created by our desire for progress. We know what destructive impact scientific and technological progress has had on the environment and the inner health of many people, and we have begun to question this. This is not to suggest that we should agree with all that de Maistre says – we cannot judge him entirely without regard for the sensibilities of our age – but it does imply that he may still have much to tell us and that we have much to learn should we be willing. If he were alive today we might expect he would quite naturally moderate his views to the milieu in which he was born. Yes, he would be a reactionary, but he would, we might suggest, fit in within the world in which he found himself. What he would provide us with, as he indeed does through the distance of years, is a template by which we might judge our place in the world. It provides us with a set of presumptions by which we can locate ourselves. De Maistre allows us to place ourselves with regard to the modern.

This begins to give us some inkling of what antimodernism might be. I wish to state that there are four key elements to antimodernism as it can be configured in the conditions that prevail in a world that is becoming sceptical of the effects of progress. Each of these elements builds on the previous ones to create an interlocking picture of antimodernism as a defensive mechanism against progress.

The first is that instead of being concerned with what is new and different we wish to *focus on the accepted and habitual ways of acting and doing*. We have a rhythm to our lives and we take this as normal and proper. This has developed over time and we have adopted it without any conscious act of will. It is not based on anything rational and is not amenable to rational assessment and critique. It is something we have inherited and accept because of who, what, and where we are. Accordingly, we will resent being pushed out of this rhythm and resist those who seek to force us to accept what is new and different. However, to return to our discussion of Oakeshottian conservatism, we can no longer maintain our complacency but feel we have no option but to react.

The second key element develops out of the first. The accepted and habitual ways of behaving lead us to believe that *there is a common culture of which we are a part*. This connects us with others around us and gives us a sense that we share something greater than ourselves. There are particular ways of behaving and responding that mean we belong to this greater whole. This common culture has come before us and will reach beyond us and this makes us a part of something with continuity and a significance that transcends our everyday concerns. This sense of allegiance, however, does not negate differences between us, nor mean that we might feel separated or even alienated from others. However, the common culture is how we feel we are tied to others and determines our response to them and, in turn, how we expect them to act with regard to us. This sense of commonality might remain implicit and appear merely as part of the accepted and habitual. However, it might become explicit if it is challenged or threatened either from within or without.

The third element takes the idea a stage further in that it stresses that *the culture remains common only by placing as a priority its transmission from one generation to the next*. One of the principal elements of a common culture is the regard for its own continuance. This is the only means by which the accepted forms of acting might be preserved and our lives continue on unchallenged. The key institutions of that culture need therefore to be geared towards its reproduction through the transmission of knowledge and understanding.

As Gordon Graham (2002) has argued in his study on the modern university, institutions like the universities are neither machines for producing graduates or isolated ivory towers existing their own sake. Universities exist to preserve and maintain a common culture. Scruton (2006) states that students exist for universities rather than the reverse. Students are receptacles for knowledge, which in due time they can then pass onto the next generation.

This takes us to the fourth and final element, in that we see *the principal aim of government as being the protection of those institutions that transmit the common culture.* The aim of government should be to maintain those institutions, traditions and practices that allow the common culture to thrive.

This view contains within it parts of Counter-Enlightenment thought: the anti-rationalism, the cultural specificity and the virtue of the old over the new. But it does so without the specific baggage of de Maistre or any other time-bound thinker. There is no call for a return to throne and altar and no paean to the executioner. What it does do is to point to the tried and trusted forms, to what has worked and what continues to do so. The things that antimodernists call for are not speculative or utopian, but are rather real traditions, structures and institutions that have worked and prospered, and whose decline, forced by the cause of progress, has caused major social and political upheavals.

These key elements also provide us with a link between the different forms of reaction we have identified. The articulate and intellectual form of reaction can be located here with its concern for the defence of a particular culture, maintaining key institutions and an argument for the proper role of government. We can readily fit the work of thinkers such as Burke and Scruton into this mould. Similarly, the more inchoate commonsense idea of reaction can be connected through its sense of a presumed common culture, based on accepted ways of acting and doing, but which is now seen as threatened by elites who continue to propose things that are new and distinct.

It is, however, in the nature of antimodernism to present its arguments negatively. It is against something – those ideas that threaten the accepted and traditional common culture – and so it will tend to present a defensive argument. And, of course, what is argued against is modernity.

Arthur Versluis (2006) argues that modernism 'is practically speaking synonymous with the mass consumerist society that is ascendant in the latter half of the twentieth century, and that places its primary faith in technological and historical progress' (p.97). We shall explore the meaning of modernity in more detail in the next section, but Versluis's definition allows us to see what is at stake for the antimodernist. He suggests that antimodernists see decline instead of progress:

> If the essence of 'modernism' is progress, a belief that technological development means socioeconomic improvement, the heart of antimodernism is a realization that 'progress' has an underbelly—that technological-industrial development has destructive consequences in three primary and intertwined areas: nature, culture, and religion. (2006, p. 97)

This extends our definition somewhat to include the decline of religion and nature as well as culture. But it is clear that there is a developing concern for the impact of scientific progress on the environment and, as we have seen, a concern for the decline of religion can be seen as far back as de Maistre in the late 18th century.

Versluis (2006) points to several different forms of antimodernism. The first he calls 'soft antimodernism' and this would include those who seek to moderate modernity and bolster tradition. He includes writers such as Hillarie Belloc and G K Chesterton, who oppose modernity on religious grounds, and T S Eliot and W B Yeats, who offered a critique of the cultural fragmentation brought in by modernity. This form of soft antimodernism operates from within the modern. It does not seek to destroy the modern world or to exile itself from it. Instead it bases its antimodernism on critique and dialogue and a call to defend what is under threat. It is this form of antimodernism that I see as most readily relating to the forms of reaction discussed in this book.

But there are other forms and Versluis distinguishes this 'soft' form with 'hard antimodernism', which consists of those who violently oppose and seek to destroy modern technological societies. These antimodernists seek to create a fundamental change; to put things back to where they were, or where the proponents imagine things were. This category, he suggests, can include certain types of Islamic extremism and other forms of direct action seeking to bring modernism down from within or without. He then goes on to discuss other forms of antimodernism, which involve extreme environmentalism, primitivists who call for a return to a pre-modern and non-industrial form of social organisation such as John Zerzan (2005, 2008), and those who seek to perpetrate acts of isolated violence against modernity such as the so called Unabomber in the US. Versluis argues that the advent of environmental concerns such as pollution and global warming have given an impetus to certain forms of antimodernism and lent it a more extremist tinge.

What is interesting is that Versluis sees antimodernism, of whatever type, as being inherently interlinked with modernism, and this relates to the connection we have made between reaction and progress. We have suggested that reaction depends on the ubiquity of calls for progress, and Versluis suggests that the same applies with the relationship between modernism and antimodernism. He points out that many of the great writers associated with modernism – Eliot, Rilke, Pound, Yeats – were actually antimodern in their outlook. These writers were concerned with the decline of traditional culture and religion caused by scientific and technological advances. He states that 'antimodernism is fundamental to the creative impulse in modernity. Modern industrial society in its very nature calls forth antimodernism in the creative individual' (p. 96). Antimodernism is here seen as the active questioning of the modernist project.

This suggests two things: that antimodernism will always exist, but also that it is always faced with the potential for contradiction. First, as Versluis (2006) states:

> we must recognize that antimodernism is not going to disappear. It cannot, because, as we have seen, it is bound up intimately, indissolubly, with modernity itself. As soon as industrialism was introduced, one saw Luddites; as soon as computers were introduced, one saw critics of computer technology. What is more, opposition to mechanized social structures is a necessary corrective, because without such opposition society is inclined to go very far, no doubt too far, in a particular direction. (2006, pp. 121-2)

So as long as there is modernism, with its call for progress, there will be those who agonise over the impact of that progress and call for it to stop, to be turned back or to be mitigated in some way.

But this suggests that there is always the potential for contradiction within antimodernism. If, as I would suggest we should, we reject the idea that we can live outside of the modern world, or that we must destroy all its vestiges, we must accept that we will always be implicated in the actions of modernity. The modern world is where we have our creature comforts and where we become dependent on particular technologies. However, these technologies bring with them the promise of advancement: we are promised ever more powerful computers, smarter mobile phones, faster broadband, more reliable cars, and so on. We have this ready sense that our accumulated store of knowledge is increasing and this is of benefit to us. This relates to the sense we have of complacency, of a ready acceptance of what we have and where we are that helps to locate us in our place in the world. We do not have to know how these things work or appreciate the science involved, we merely want them and expect them to work. We may disagree with aspects of how we are governed and the state of the country; we may point to particular policies and actions by politicians that we abhor, but what we do not object to is the materialism and comforts of the modern world.

Accordingly, we do not acknowledge that it is the existence of these technologies that might add to the sense of malaise we have with respect to the modern world. We might expect the 24-hour media that allows us to know much more about what is going on and is there seemingly at our convenience. But it is these very integrated technologies that allow bankers to use virtual money to real effect, creating profits and debt and to burden themselves and others with risk. The financial crisis of 2007-8 was partly a product of the technologies we take for granted. Similarly, the very ease of travel, which we take advantage of for our foreign holidays and business trips, allows economic migrants easy access to our country and contributes to climate change. The material quality of modern life allows us to live well, and we wish this to remain. The problem is whether we can connect this to the sense of malaise we might have, and then be prepared to do something about it, especially if it means some form of sacrifice on our part.

This is where there is a division between the different forms of reaction, between the articulate and concerned critics of modernity, and those who adopt a commonsense reaction against certain aspects of the modern world that seem to confront them from time to time. Some reactionary critics, such as the Prince of Wales (2010), René Guénon (2001b, 2001c) and Seyyed Hossein Nasr (1997) are highly critical of Western materialism. As we shall see, these critics take issue with the manner in which the modern world is dominated by materialistic values, with what Guénon (2001c, 2001e,) refers to as quantity rather than quality, and with the temporal rather than the spiritual. However, we would have to suggest that the commonsense critique of the modern world we have discussed in the previous chapter appears to lack any clamour for a spiritual revival at the expense of our material affluence. This does not mean that it is content with the modern world, but rather than the discontent is caused by different, and more specific, aspects of modernity.

This further amplifies a point we have stressed already: that not only are there different forms of reaction, that have different targets, it might actually be the case that different forms of reaction are in conflict with each other. So, for example, the commonsense view of reaction might not find the Prince of Wales' arguments for a turn away from industrial and therefore cheap food production and high-energy usage congenial. Likewise, as we have seen, there are obvious conflicts between European reaction, with its emphasis on national identity and the preservation of tradition, and Islamic reaction with its desire to spread the word of Islam and even to restore the Caliphate (Fallaci, 2002, 2006).

One of the fascinating aspects of this diversity of reaction is that it is not absurd, indeed not unusual, for progressives to come out in support of certain forms of reaction. We saw this with radicals like Michel Foucault who, in 1979, supported the Iranian revolution. However, more recently we see that some on the left have made links with Islamic fundamentalists because of their common cause over the Iraq war and the Israeli-Palestine conflict. Nor, as we have seen, is it completely odd to talk of a type of 'liberal reaction' as shown by politicians such as Pym Fortuyn and Gert

Wilders (although we might question whether this form of reaction can properly be called antimodern).

So antimodernism, like reaction, will take many forms and it would be a mistake to see it as a consistent and coherent entity. There are those who seek to destroy modernity and all its creations and replace it with a distinctly different form of social organisation. This hard form of antimodernism is not the form we wish to develop here. Instead we wish to follow the form developed from within modernism, which seeks to question and to spread doubt and suspicion about those ideas and concepts that are the core of modernity. Our aim is not to destroy, but then nor is it to create. We seek only to question and so delay. To be antimodern is to focus on the past, on heritage, on harmony, and on our connection with tradition. It is to pay due regard to civility, and to the need to complement what already exists rather than to replace it. Antimodernism gives regard to what has gone before and to give it a higher place than the instant, and quite probably temporary, constructions of the present. To be antimodern is to be, as a matter of practice, continually learning from the past. We see that the past is the best possible teacher: it is better than any abstract theory and to be preferred to the utopianism of the moderns.

III

But just what is it that antimodernists object to? Following O'Hear's distinction between the Enlightenment and Counter-Enlightenment we can suggest that the modern is indeed the belief in progress and that solutions to social and political problems are possible through the application of reason. It therefore places a premium on the idea of change and sees the need for flux and constant adaptation. This presupposes a desire always to look forwards and to reject the past, the idea of tradition and established forms of behaviour in favour of an objective and supposedly scientific approach to problem solving. This carries with it the positivistic notion that problems can be correctly identified and solutions posited and implemented by experts who have the requisite expertise and knowledge, something that is denied to the ordinary person. The modernist believes that there is a body of knowledge, based on first principles that can be applied to social and political problems.

So the idea of the modern is more than meaning simply the world as it is now. Instead it is concerned with a particular rationalist approach to the world that sees human perfectibility as a necessary aim and that this can be achieved through the application of scientific or technical means. It involves the placing of innovation and newness over tradition. Indeed, as with the Enlightenment, it will tend to involve the general denigration of traditional practices and reject the past as a guide for future action. It will tend to neglect our ancestors and the old established ways of doing things in favour of innovation and the original.

This suggests that modernity will be self-regarding and will refuse to look at aspects of the world that do not fit into its template of progress and innovation. It believes in its own superiority and that it need not look outside of its own methods of analysis to discover facts about the world. This flows from the conceit that we moderns are inevitably superior to our ancestors and that our duty is to ensure that this ascendency continues: we are more advanced than those who preceded us and we understand more about the world than they did. We therefore do not need to respect the past and tradition, whether it is in politics, our history, high culture, architecture and so on. Scruton (1994) talks of the disrespect and incivility of modern architecture and design, where buildings do not complement their surroundings, or seek to fit in. Instead they seek to make their own statement, to stress their individuality divorced from any context, their immediate environment and the traditions of the past.

Of course, the primary example of this is the comment of Le Corbusier (1927) that 'A house is a machine for living in' (p. 95). Le Corbusier felt that the mechanical metaphor was generally applicable to modernity, and thus his model of housing could and should apply in all cases. Modern human beings therefore have no other context than their modernity. Their needs could now be expressed free of geography, history, caste or creed. All these factors were deemed irrelevant in the face of modernity; Le Corbusier took it for granted that 'All men have the same needs' (1927, p. 135). Accordingly, the aim of Le Corbusier, as with other modernists, was to remove any specificity from their architecture, to decouple it from its local environment. We can see this when we look at Le Corbusier's *Une Petite Maison*, a house he designed for his mother on the shores of Lake Geneva in 1923-4 (Baltanás, 2005). As José Baltanás states, this house 'asserted the autonomy of modern architecture over the impositions of the site' (2005, p. 37). What this means is that Le Corbusier made no attempt, and saw no need, to blend his architecture in with the local surroundings. It was rather the case that the site should be made to fit the design.

This decontextualisation is further emphasised by the fact that the house was later covered in corrugated aluminium cladding

> of the type used in the construction of the fuselage of planes. It hardly need be pointed out that this modification was entirely to the liking of Le Corbusier, as it emphasised the metaphor of the house as a machine. (Baltanás, 2005, p. 38)

Consequently, the house, which sits right on the shore of Lake Geneva and offers truly stunning views across the lake, has the external appearance of a flat-roofed barn or cow shed, its incongruity matched only by its ugliness. As a piece of architecture it can only be appreciated by viewing it without any context and without questioning how it fits into the site. This, however, was the primary aim of modernism: to reduce all to its own concerns.

Modernism, as an intellectual movement, developed from post-Reformation and Enlightenment concerns to develop objective science and a universal morality and laws. These were seen to be autonomous systems of thought in the sense of operating according to their own inner logic rather than being circumscribed by external pressures (Harvey, 1989). It was thus the belief that one could construct a better world and improve humanity through the active pursuit of rationality, objectivity and a universal morality. There is within this an explicit belief in progress towards a particular purpose, the pursuit of which was necessarily universal as it was deemed to lead to an improvement in the human condition. According to David Harvey, the Enlightenment project, 'took it as axiomatic that there was only one possible answer to any question' (1989, p.27). It involved 'the belief in linear progress, absolute truths, and rational planning of ideal social orders under standardised conditions of knowledge and production' (1989, p.35). The means of achieving this was through the adoption of a rational scientific epistemic towards the so-called 'human sciences' of sociology, politics, economics, etc. These emerging disciplines become the vehicles for describing progress towards 'ideal social orders'.

The Enlightenment project was aimed at secularisation, placing rational thought and science over and above religious explanations of the human situation. Yet as both John Gray (1993) and Anthony O'Hear (1999) have pointed out, the very fact that Enlightenment thinkers sought to create ideal social orders reintroduced a version of Christian eschatology to modern thought. Gray's critique of progress is particularly relevant to our discussion here, showing the self-contradictory nature of modern calls for progress. He argues that we lack the means to measure progress and improvement in human affairs. But he goes further than this. Gray argues that 'the idea of progress is particularly pernicious when it acts to suppress awareness of mystery and tragedy in human life' (1993, p. 138). He feels that peddling the idea that life will be better in the future, and that sacrifices and suffering by people today are therefore worthwhile, 'corrupts our perception of human life, in which the fate of each individual is – for him or her – an ultimate fact, which no improvement in the life of the species can alter or redeem' (p. 139). We are, so to speak, equal under God and so no one life can be used for the purpose of furthering the project of another.

Gray also suggests that 'the project of universal improvement' (p. 139) can be questioned in that 'the eradication of one evil typically spawns others, and many goods are dependent for their existence on evils' (p. 139). In other words we cannot know what effect our efforts at improvement might have and whether they will actually make our lives better or worse. Gray also agrees with anti-enlightenment thinkers such as Herder, who question the commensurability of concepts of the good and so argue it is incoherent to talk about making progress. In other words, if there is no such things as a universal good that applies to all cultures, how can we state that progress is being, or even can be, made?

Lastly, Gray sees progress as a 'surrogate for spiritual meaning' (p. 139), which encourages us to see our lives 'not under the aspect of eternity, but as moments in a universal process of betterment' (p. 139). Instead of living for now and accepting our place in the world and our life as it is, we instead are always looking forward to what we might become. Gray argues that 'the idea of progress reinforces the restless discontent that is one of the diseases of modernity' (p. 139). We are never content with our lot, but instead are constantly striving for that which is always just beyond us.

So we can suggest that the utopian element within calls for progress owed much to the religious impulse, or what Eric Voegelin (1987) rather unhelpfully termed the immanentisation of the eschaton. According to Voegelin (1987, 1997), utopian thought integrated much of the millennial tendencies of pre-renaissance Christianity. It integrated into its thinking the idea that the Second Coming was imminent and so sacrifices were worth the making.

Jean Francois Lyotard (1984) describes the term 'modern' in terms of the development of the human sciences, which he refers to as 'metadiscourses'. He defines a metadiscourse as a 'discourse of legitimation with respect to its own status' (1984, pxxiii). It is a justificatory explanation of its own purpose as discourse. It seeks to provide a justification for the imposition of a particular means to truth. According to Lyotard such metadiscourses make 'an explicit appeal to some grand narrative, such as the dialectics of Spirit, the hermeneutics of meaning, the emancipation of the rational or working subject, or the creation of wealth' (1984, pxxiii). These metanarratives are attempts to develop a total vision of human progress. They are the means to achieving an 'ideal social order', whether it be based on Hegel's idealism, Marxism or capitalism. According to Lyotard, these are all examples of grand purposive visions of human progress towards utopia.

Lyotard sees modernism as creating bodies of scientific knowledge aimed at a total description of human beings and identifying a means of achieving the ideal, be it the end of history, or the classless society. The expert, with the requisite knowledge gleaned from the properly developed human sciences is capable of plotting a path towards the achievement of important social goals.

Therefore, a key part of modernism, particularly as it is applied to the social and political context, is that it is possible to place the human sciences on the same level as the natural sciences. This has become known as positivism, which can be defined as the acceptance by social scientists of the empiricist account of the natural sciences. This is the belief that knowledge can only be gained through the systematic observation of the world. Science is based on direct observation of phenomena rather than through reasoning or independent conjecture. As Benton and Craib (2001) have suggested, it is the belief that 'science is valued as the highest or even the only genuine form of knowledge' and that the 'scientific method can and should be extended to the study of human mental and social life, to establish these disciplines as social *sciences*' (p. 23) They go on to state that 'Once reliable social scientific knowledge has been established, it will be possible to apply it to control, or regulate the behaviour of individuals or groups in society' (p. 23). The answers to problems can be identified and resolved by the application of this knowledge on the part of experts in the same manner as in the natural sciences and engineering. Technical solutions to problems are eminently possible and they should be sought. This approach places great authority in the hands of scientists. They are portrayed as the experts able to disperse their knowledge to solve social problems.

So modernism can be described as the belief in progress towards a particular end. Whilst the end may differ, as between Marxist and capitalist conceptions of progress, the epistemic of scientific and rational progress is not questioned. But these, of course, are now seen as highly questionable notions. Marxism, after Stalin, Mao and Pol Pot, cannot be so readily equated with progress, and the Anglo-Saxon model of capitalism, based on global financial markets, cannot necessarily be taken as a model way forward. Modern architecture can no longer be seen as meeting the needs of humanity trumpeted by Le Corbusier. Indeed it was in architecture that an alternative to modernism first made some headway.

IV

One could argue that one of the reasons for the scepticism towards the modernist project is its ahistorical, universally prescriptive nature. It seemed to suggest that there was one universally applicable solution that could be applied regardless of context and culture. Hence Le Corbusier (1927) could assert that his form of architecture met the needs of humanity and could be applied in any place where there was a client sufficiently sensible to employ him. Charles Jencks (1989) saw that this hubris was all of a part with modernism's desire to centralise processes in order to try and control mass production and mass culture. The belief in homogeneous universal solutions necessitated the need to control the environment and the community in order to facilitate these solutions. The result was architecture that failed to meet the needs of its users and even seemed to ignore them or insist that they modify their behaviour to suit the building.

It was from criticisms such as these that what became referred to as postmodernism developed. Postmodernism was a reaction against the universal modernist vision of the world. It was against the belief in absolute truths. It found that the whole idea that we could plan rationally to create the ideal social order deeply problematical. It also took issue with the standardisation of knowledge (Harvey 1989). Postmodernism could be seen then as a reaction against the concept of 'Man' and marked a return to the notion of the person.

Postmodernism first manifested itself as a movement in architecture with a return to vernacular styles and with pluralism in planning to create a 'collage' of 'differentiated spaces' rather than attempting to achieve 'grandiose plans based on functional zoning of different activities' (Harvey, 1989; p.46).

Postmodernism, instead of offering one total solution, is rather what Jencks has referred to as a form of 'double-coding'. It is 'fundamentally the eclectic mixture of any tradition with that of the immediate past' (1989, p.7). It looks to certain traditions and seeks to mix these with elements of modernism, particularly its technology. Jencks sees postmodernism as a 'paradoxical dualism' that involves the continuation of modernism and its transcendence. Postmodern architects maintain certain of the methods of modernism, but it is merely one tradition – the most recent – and deserving no greater attention than another. Rather postmodernism is a mixing of styles and traditions in order to achieve something distinctive. It is a return to the attempt to reference architecture within a tradition rather than attempting to create an abstract universal ideal.

The concern for pluralism recognises that communities are diverse and diffuse in their interests, traditions and styles. Indeed the world is segmented and decentralised with an increasing political and cultural regionalism where differences matter and are worth defending (Jencks 1989). Postmodernism recognises what is termed 'the other', as a recognition of the rights of other people who should have the same opportunities as us. This suggests a similarity with the cultural particularism and specificity that we saw as part of the Counter-Enlightenment. Instead of modernism's universalism, the postmodern, like the early critics of the modern, seek to emphasise the diversity and differences of particular cultures.

But postmodernism can be seen as referring to more than just architecture. The term is now perceived as a more general description of a cultural shift away from homogeneity to contextualisation, and from universality to localism. In philosophical terms postmodernism has been described as 'incredibility towards metanarratives' (Lyotard, 1984; pxxiv). As we have seen, Lyotard sought to question the idea of the metanarrative, the total, universally applicable solution. Accordingly, postmodernism is here seen to represent the absolute implausibility of these totalising visions of human progress. It is a recognition that we cannot simply rely on the expert or the technician with their scientific knowledge.

Lyotard argues that knowledge has become more diffuse and, importantly, diffusing. Knowledge no longer simply serves the interests of an elite, but can come to the service of us all. He states that, 'Postmodern knowledge is not simply a tool of the authorities; it refines our sensitivity to differences and reinforces our ability to tolerate the incommensurable' (1984, pxxv). So a postmodern description is aware of divergence and difference – of 'otherness'. However, instead of attempting to minimise this otherness and mould it into a universal pattern, postmodernism seeks to enhance this difference.

According to Lyotard, postmodernism is a move away from abstract theorising towards a celebration of life as it is lived. As such it appreciates contingency, uncertainty, the marginal and the excluded (Sarup, 1988). It can thus be perceived as a shift from universal ends to local or personal means. The question, Lyotard tells us, now being asked is not 'Is it true?', but rather 'What use is it?' (Lyotard 1984; p. 51). It is a shift away from an intrinsic characterisation — of what a thing is — to what it does in people's lives. An object is not something with intrinsic qualities, but rather its qualities reside in how it allows us to fulfil our own purposes. Its purpose is thus relational to use, not to a 'truth' described through the idealised ends of modernism.

There is an apparent similarity here to the antimodern critique of modernism. Postmodernism involves a double-coding whereby tradition is referenced and applied. However, it is not being used for itself — because it is a tradition that we wish to preserve because of how we view it — but it is integrated into a framework combining modernist techniques. The reference to tradition, therefore, may be ironic, rather than a sincere attempt to place tradition at the centre of things.

There may be virtues in this use of traditions. First, it might be seen as anti-elitist, in that it rejects the totalising vision of the expert and seeks to relate to how people actually have, and currently do, live and think. It might be seen as a return to recognisability and context. Second, it seeks to be more understandable, because of this very recognisability. Third, it aims to be more localised through referencing to historical links. There is no imposition of a general or universal standard; rather types of provision are related to local context. Thus the postmodern concern for tradition relates to local meanings. There may then be linkages here to the concerns of commonsense reaction, which, as we have seen, concerns itself with the accepted ways of doing things rather than the abstractions of an elite.

So, both antimodernism and postmodernism are critiques of modernism. But are there any real connections between them? Might they really be the same thing, but under different names to avoid any link with reaction? Marxist critics, such as David Harvey (1989) and Frederick Jameson (1992), certainly argue that postmodernism is merely another means of protecting capitalism, through a shift from an ideology based on production to one concerned with consumption. In that sense it is merely a means in which a form of modernism seeks to preserve itself in the face of globalisation and the failed experiments of the recent past.

But we should be cautious of the connection between these two critiques of modernity. First, we should examine the difference in names. Antimodernism is against the modern: it seeks to fight it, to replace it or to significantly moderate it. However, the ambition of postmodernists is to go beyond the modern: they are what comes after or supersedes the modern. It is not then so much a reaction against anything as a move beyond, or perhaps even a development out of, the modern. They are not, strictly speaking, opposed to modernity, but rather they see themselves as coming after, and as a result of, the modern. It is therefore not a return to the past, even if it might mix some ingredients of traditions with modern technology as Charles Jencks has argued. So, while there are apparent similarities between postmodernists and the Counter-Enlightenment, such as the importance of cultural differences and the rejection of grand theory that we see in thinkers such as Edmund Burke (1999b), there are important differences. In particular, we can suggest that postmodernism retains the hubris and conceited ambition of modernism. It still seeks to create something new and distinctive, something that is different from what has gone before. Postmodernism still places a premium on originality. It does not seek to reject the modern, but rather it seeks to take it further and develop it into a new and unique vision. So, while the postmodern does not ignore the past, nor does it use it with respect. It abuses the past, twisting it to its own ironic ends, and as a result creates kitsch or pastiche. It creates parodies of traditional forms, rather than constructing with integrity and honesty.

So even though postmodernism ostensibly rejects the grand narratives of modernity, it does not deny the latter's search for the new and the different. What is distinctive about postmodernism is that it has rejected any sense of purpose. It does not concern itself with progress. Instead postmodernism tends to be almost entirely concerned with self-reference and it has extended the incivility of modernism to this aim. Hence the rise of star architects like Frank Gehry, Zaha Hadid, Rem Koolhaas and Daniel Libeskind, who for all their flair and distinctiveness, really just seem to be building for themselves. They seek to be making a statement of their originality: to be different, distinct, to stand out and be seen as groundbreaking, is now the main concern of architecture. Difference becomes an end in itself. The star architect is always seeking to move on, to create the new, to be original, to create the iconic building, but for no other purpose than they have the capability of doing so. There is no attempt here to change the world, to improve humanity or society, or even to preserve a tradition, but rather just to make a personal statement, to create and maintain celebrity. *Postmodernism is not an attempt to make a difference, but just to be different.*

In this way it is indeed distinctly different from the antimodern. In a sense, while postmodernism ostensibly rejects the idea of progress, it merely seeks to democratise it. It reduces social action to individual choice and the opportunity for celebrity. We might suggest that it maintains all that is worrying about modernism, particularly its desire for flux and change, but denies that this has any purpose other than its own perpetuation.

This suggests that we can accept elements of the critique provided by postmodernism, but we have to be cautious about adopting it as a model. It does not provide the reactionary with any means to deal with the modern. We should, therefore, perhaps accept the view of Marxist critics such as David Harvey, and see the postmodernism as merely another stage of the modern, as an attempt to retain some plausibility for the claims of progress and change. It is then something quite different from the antimodern, and we cannot rely on it to bolster the reactionary critique of modernity.

V

Both antimodernism and postmodernism make a claim in favour of tradition. But are they really talking about the same thing? Postmodernists talk of a 'double-coding' where they seek to meld the techniques of modernism with other traditions to create something knowingly ironic. The aim here is not especially to preserve a particular tradition, but to use it to create an effect. For the postmodernist, tradition is a particular custom or practice that is used by a particular culture. It has some meaning through being handed down over the generations, and so has some particular utility within that culture or community. This means that we can talk of traditions, or a multiplicity of cultural practices all with their specific resonance within a given community. The postmodernist can therefore choose from this body of traditions in order to create a particular effect.

But this is only one way in which tradition is viewed. Instead of seeing the term in the plural, of there being many traditions, we can talk of tradition in the singular. This is where it a specific thing or rather a set of universal principles that underpin all modern religions and systems of thought. Accordingly, the perennial philosopher, René Guénon talks of tradition and of traditionalism. This does not take tradition as a set of local customs and practices, but as the primordial basis of all ancient thought.

Guénon's thought is useful to us here because of its explicit antimodernism and the manner in which it shows up the conceit of progress. Therefore, we should consider traditionalism precisely because it provides such a complete critique of modernity, which links back to many of the concerns of the Counter-Enlightenment. What makes it interesting is that, even though Guénon contrasts the West unfavourably with the East, traditionalism is a creation of the West and speaks to westerners. It is perhaps the most comprehensive contemporary reaction to modernity from within modernity itself. As Mark Sedgwick (2004) shows, the main target for traditionalism is the modern world and its infatuation with progress and change as an end in itself: it is explicitly set against modernity.

In a sense all of the major religions consider themselves to be 'the' tradition, in that they suggest a monopoly of truth, or they hold the keys to the door to truth. However, perennialists like Guénon argue that there is a primordial system of thought, which he calls tradition, which underpins all these faiths. It is therefore deeper than any of the ancient religions even as they take elements from its store of wisdom. Guénon argues that much of this wisdom has been lost in the West and in its place is the shallow belief in material progress.

Sedgwick (2004) shows that the Latin root of 'traditions' is *tradere,* which means to hand over or hand down. It can be taken to mean a 'belief and practice transmitted (especially orally) from generation to generation' (p. 21). But what matters with tradition is just what is being handed down. Several of Guénon's followers have sought to clarify precisely what he meant by tradition. For example, Robin Waterfield (2002) states that

> Tradition was essentially the body of knowledge and self-understanding which is common to all men in all ages and nationalities. Its expression and clarification forms the basis of all traditional wisdom and its application the basis of all traditional societies. (p. 80)

Tradition is a body of knowledge that is potentially open to all and which forms the basis for all wisdom. It is the manner in which we can come to understand the world that we are in. As Luc Benoist (2003) states

> It is concerned with origins: tradition is the handing on of a complex of established means for facilitating our understanding of the immanent principles of universal order, since it has not been granted mankind to understand unaided the meaning of his existence. (p. 14)

Benoist suggests that tradition is akin to the 'spiritual relationship between a master and pupil, that it to say of a formative influence analogous to that of spiritual vocation or inspiration, as actual for the spirit as heredity is for the body' (p. 14). He goes on:

> What we are concerned with here is an inner knowledge, co-existent with life itself; a coexistent reality, but at the same time an awareness of a superior consciousness, recognised as such, and at this level inseparable from the person it has brought to birth and for whom it constitutes the raison d'être.
>
> From this point of view the person is completely what he transmits, he only is in what he transmits, and in the degree to which he *does* transmit. Independence and individuality are thus seen to be relative realities only, which bear witness to our progressive separation and continuous falling away from the

> possession of an all-embracing original wisdom, a wisdom that is quite compatible with an archaic way of life. (p. 14)

As we move away from this wisdom, the more obscure it becomes and so we find it harder to understand the true nature of ancient civilisations. We become incapable of seeing the essential unity, the basic inclusiveness of tradition. So tradition is a particular type of wisdom, which forms the basis for all human understanding.

Guénon is critical of what he always refers to as the West. The basis for his critique is that the West has now forgotten the ancient wisdom: it has lost its connection to tradition. In its place has been put progress and the belief that the West is superior because of its apparent material wealth. Accordingly, his first book, *An Introduction to the Study of the Hindu Doctrines* (Guénon, 2001a; argues that

> Europeans, since the days when they began to believe in 'progress' and in 'evolution', that is to say since a little more than a century ago [he wrote this is 1921], profess to see a sign of inferiority in this absence of change, whereas, for our part, we look upon it as a balanced condition which Western civilisation has failed to achieve. Moreover, this stability shows itself in small things as well as in great; a striking example of this is to be found in the fact that 'fashion', with its continual changes, is only to be met with in the West. In short, Westerners, and especially modern Westerners, appear to be endowed with changeable and inconsistent natures, hankering after movement and excitement, whereas the Eastern nature shows quite the opposite characteristics. (p. 13)

Guénon locates progress as a product of the late 17th and early 18th centuries, just as de Maistre and the other contemporary Counter-Enlightenment critics did. This has come about because the West has diverged from the East, and the main causes of this are the Renaissance and the Reformation, which destroyed the last vestiges of ancient tradition in Europe. Guénon (2001d) argues that the Renaissance 'was in reality not a re-birth but the death of many things' (p. 15). Much of the traditional sciences of the Middle Ages were lost, and in its place there was only 'profane' science and 'profane' philosophy. The decline of the West reached its nadir with the French Revolution, which completely rejected all tradition.

Like the antimodernists of the Counter-Enlightenment, Guénon, in what is perhaps his most influential work, *East and West* (2001b), argues that there are many forms of civilisation, not just the one, as Europeans believe. Indeed the West is the odd one out in comparison to all other civilisations:

> The civilization of the modern West appears in history as a veritable anomaly: among all those which are known to us more or less completely, this civilization is the only one that has developed along purely material lines, and this monstrous development, whose beginnings coincide with the Renaissance, has been accompanied, as indeed it was fated to be, by a corresponding intellectual regress. (p. 11)

He goes on:

> This regress has reached such a point that the Westerners of today no longer know what pure intellect is; in fact they do not even suspect that anything of the kind can exist; hence their disdain, not only for Eastern civilization, but also for the Middle Ages of Europe, whose spirit escapes them scarcely less completely. (p. 11)

What Guénon finds most preposterous is that the West thinks that it is the main form of civilisation. He is contemptuous of the idea that it alone deserves to be called a civilisation because it can boast of progress. Instead he sees progress, and the growth of materialism that became linked to it in the second half of the 18th century, as a 'substitute for thought' (p. 16) and useful for 'imposing upon a mob' (p. 16). Progress had no substance, and was based on no higher principle than itself, even though progress was seen as indefinite. For Guénon, 'What Westerners call progress is for nothing but change and instability'. (p. 26)

Sedgwick (2004) argues that in *East and West* Guénon 'systematically attacks the illusion of materialism and the "superstitions" of progress, reason, change (as desirable in itself), and sentimental moralizing (an Anglo-Saxon specialty)' (p. 25). However, Sedgwick believes that: 'What Guénon opposes is not the West but the modern world' (p. 25). He does not wish to see the West superseded by the East, but instead seeks to restore an appropriate Western civilisation. As a civilisation it had lost its real, namely, spiritual foundations, and what was needed was an intellectual elite to help build these foundations anew. This, we might suggest, is the purpose of Guénon's life's work.

Indeed, as Robin Waterfield (2002) states: 'East and West are not primarily geographical or even cultural distinctions; they are symbols of two different fundamental attitudes towards reality' (p. 69). The West, 'especially during the last 600 years ... has concentrated the greater part of its attention on the phenomenal world of matter', while the East 'has concentrated on the transcendent reality accessible only to man by direct intellectual intuition' (p. 69). Guénon wished to shift the balance in the West back towards this 'transcendent reality'.

Guénon develops his critique of modernity in a sequel to *East and West* entitled *The Crisis of the Modern World* (Guénon, 2001c). In this work he criticises humanism and the move toward the secular or the profane. This is a theme he refers to again and again in his work, seeking to rebalance the sacred and the profane. He believed that proper government would be spiritual rather than temporal (see also Guénon, 2001d). This meant that Guénon had a low regard for democracy and the popular will, seeing that those ignorant of tradition could not direct a society. It was not, he argued, possible for a lower principle to determine a higher one, and as such democracy was deeply flawed.

But he was also critical of individualism – and the fact that in modern society there appeared to be 'the negation of any principle higher than individuality, and the consequent reduction of civilization, in all its branches, to purely human elements' (2001c, p. 55). This placing of the individual above all else meant that material conditions prevailed and novelty and personal satisfaction became the motive forces of Western societies. Guénon contrasted this with a traditional society where the will of the individual would be sublimated into the whole: 'In a traditional civilization it is almost inconceivable that a man should claim an idea as his own' (2001c, p. 56). Waterfield (2002) backs up this criticism of individualism when he states that 'the idea of novelty and originality so very much prized by modern Westerners' is 'scarcely more than two hundred years old. Fewer still realize, as Guénon did, how false, and consequently harmful, it is'. (p. 78)

A key problem with the modern world according to Guénon is the manner in which religion has become denigrated. In *Symbols of Sacred Science* (Guénon, 2001f) he argues that a key part of the decline of the West has been the relegation of religion to merely a social phenomenon, whereby is becomes seen as separate from other parts of the culture. It is just another aspect of the culture, rather than something upon which civilisation itself depends upon.

We can see much here that is familiar in our discussion on both antimodernism and reaction. Indeed, from Guénon's perspective a traditionalist must be antimodern. He could not conceive of traditionalism reconciling itself with the modern world. However, he did not believe that we should seek to destroy the West and nor did he believe we could turn the clock back or step off the world. Instead, as Waterfield (2002) points out, 'we can see clearly the way in which we are all infected with the current Western ataxia and endeavour to bring our own actions into conformity with the natural social order' (p. 85). We are part of the West, and we have been infected with this particular modern virus. What we must do is to inoculate ourselves against it, and this is the main function of the elite that Guénon sees as essential.

Despite having a considerable body of work that is now available in English, Guenon and his ideas have had little influence in mainstream academic circles (Sedgwick, 2004), although he is becoming more widely quoted particularly in his homeland, France, and in the literature on Islam in the West. Most certainly there is a literature that considers him, but his views are not in the mainstream of philosophy, theology or cultural criticism. Where he is considered, there is a tendency to put him at the extreme. For example, in Göran Dahl's work on so-called 'radical conservatism' (Dahl, 1999), he is lumped together with the Italian extreme antimodernist, Julius Evola[12], even though Dahl is conscious to make the distinction between the politics of the two. But despite this, Dahl discusses their ideas as being essentially the same and does not point out the key differences between the two thinkers over issues such as temporal versus spiri-

[12] See the brief discussion of Evola in Chapter one. I discuss Dahl's work more fully in the next chapter.

tual authority and knowledge versus action. Both were clearly antimodernists, but Evola, unlike Guénon, openly supported fascism in both Italy and Germany and was openly racist and anti-Semitic. Evola (2002) saw himself as a radical traditionalist, a form of words that one would not find coming from Guénon, who consistently placed knowledge above action (Guénon, 2001c). Indeed, Guénon was insistent on distancing himself from Evola's political activism and was critical of his attempt to desacralise tradition (Sedgwick, 2004).

There is much we can take much from Guénon's critique of modernity. In particular, his description of modernity and progress as a descent rather than advance is an important point. He provides some clear sense that there is much that is lost by progress, and that the material, which is often all that progress seems to be able to guarantee, offers only a shallow form of life. Guénon strips away the veneer of glamour from progress and shows that it is little more than selfish calculation. In this regard he provides antimodernism with a considerable depth.

VI

But not everyone can be as certain as Guénon. There is, we might say, an ambivalence in reaction and antimodernism. While antimodernists seek to oppose the modern, unlike postmodernists they realise they cannot go beyond it. They do not wish to attain some state beyond or after the modern. They would prefer a situation where they could return to a time before modernism. But also most antimodernists know, whether they admit it openly or not, that they cannot get before modernity either. We cannot undo the present and return to a past unsullied by the fetish for progress. Indeed, I would suggest, that many antimodernists – those that Arthur Versluis (2006) has referred to as 'soft' – would actually not wish to do so. They are aware that all change, in whatever direction, is unpredictable and fraught with danger. Instead, they sit within the modern and seek to criticise, to argue and to sow suspicion in the hope that some elements of the culture they see threatened can be preserved. They might even hope, like the little Dutch boy of legend, that if they keep their finger long enough in the dyke that others will come along and repair the leak before all the water is lost. They work to persuade their fellows of the risks of progress, but do not seek to bring down the whole modern edifice, quite the contrary.

So we might suggest that what reactionaries seek to achieve is something of a moderation of modernity. They wish to calm it down and reduce its most alienating and destructive effects. These might be excessive consumerism and materialism, over-consumption of the world's resources, or it be being out of harmony with nature. But in doing so, many do not seek merely to return to the past or to take a Luddite approach to modernity and its technologies, but rather to take up the know-how and capability of the present and to turn it to more benign purposes (and it is precisely that there is a purpose – to preserve – that distinguishes this from the postmodern double-coding we have considered above). This seems to be the position of the Prince of Wales in his book *Harmony* (2010). This is presented as the Prince's personal philosophical statement, and it is clear that he has been influenced deeply by traditionalist thinking. He is critical of Western culture and its materialism and wishes to encourage a transformation to what he sees as a more sustainable relationship with nature. Indeed, what he calls for is a 'sustainability revolution' (p. 3).

The book begins with an explanation of the Prince's forty-year commitment to this critique of modernity:

> My concern from the very start was that Western culture was accelerating away from values and a perspective that had, up until then, been embedded in its traditional roots. The industrialization of life was becoming comprehensive and Nature had become 'secularized'. I could see very clearly that we were growing numb to the sacred presence that all traditional societies still feel very deeply. In the West that sense of the sacred was one of the values that had stood the test of time and had helped to guide countless generations to understand the significance of Nature's processes and to live by her cyclical economy. But, like the children who followed the Pied Piper, it was as if our beguiling machines, not to say four centuries of increasingly being dependent upon a very narrow form of scientific rationalism, has led us along a new but dangerously unknown road – and a dance that has been so merry that we failed to notice how far we were being taken from our rightful home. The net result was that our culture seemed to be paying less

> and less heed to what had always been understood about the way nature worked and the limits of her benevolence, and to how, as a consequence, the subtle balance in many areas of human endeavour was being destroyed. What I could see then was that without those traditional 'anchors' our civilization would find itself in an increasingly difficult and exposed position. And, regrettably, that it what has happened. (2010, p. 15)

He believes that many others share this view. He suggests there is a general disaffection: 'I sense a growing unease and anxiety in people's souls – an unease that still remains largely unexpressed because of the understandable fear of being thought 'irrational', 'old-fashioned', 'anti-science', or 'anti-progress' (p. 27). This is an enlightening quote in that he seems to suggest that what holds people back from a more explicit support of the Prince's antimodernism is an awareness of how it might appear to the progressive consensus of elite discourse. The Prince is acknowledging the power of progressive discourse as a means of stifling debate and appearing to suggest a consensus. This, we might suggest, is an at least tacit acknowledgement of the idea of common sense reaction by the Prince.

In developing his argument, the Prince wants to show 'just how fundamentally at odds with reality our modern view has become compared with the one that sustained the world for thousands of years' (p. 83). He believes that 'we are travelling along a very wrong road' (p. 83). He wishes to suggest that human societies have moved away from a more traditional and harmonious relationship with nature, and the cause of this is modernity. A key target for him is what he terms the 'mechanistic thinking' (p. 20) of modernity. He describes this as reductionist, where nature is seen as a machine, and organisms seen only in mechanical terms: 'Hence in schools today children are generally taught to see the human heart as nothing more than a pump' (p. 20).

His view of the development of modernity follows that which we have outlined briefly above. With the advent of a scientific worldview, nature became objectified, and so began to be seen as separate from us. We were not part of nature, but rather it was a series of distinct objects that offers certain possibilities for our development. Accordingly, humans came to believe they had the right to 'manipulate and exploit every element of the natural world for the betterment of mankind' (p. 156).

But the Prince is also critical of the manner in which modernism has developed with regard to art and design and architecture. It has, the Prince suggests, 'rejected both history and Nature as central sources for design. Instead they focussed on technology and abstraction, legitimizing a kind of mythology of industrialization' (p. 169). Art and architecture no longer take their references from nature, but from an industrial aesthetic and a rationalist abstraction that has no direct connection with the outside world.

The Prince of Wales' ideas can therefore be seen as an example of antimodernism. His response has been to campaign against certain activities, such as industrial-scale agriculture and modern architecture, and to use his own resources to provide examples of alternatives to modernism, such as the development of the town of Poundbury and organic methods on his farmland.

The Prince, then, is critical of modernity and what he calls its reductive or mechanistic view of scientific progress. However, he does not reject all elements of modern science. He welcomes the advances that science has made to our health and standard of living. Likewise, in his desire to deal with man-made climate change and the over-use of the earth's resources he is prepared to accept the scientific consensus. He puts this critique of modernity and science within the context of the need to revitalise the ancient sacred traditions of the world and to return to a more harmonious balance with Nature. But his solution is entirely based on the assumptions of modern science. He apparently believes that current climate science, based presumably on the same assumptions as other scientific and technological advances, is correct in its forecasts and predictions. In other words, he chooses to trust science when it appears to confirm his views about humanity and nature, but not when it is apparently at odds with them.

But is this acceptable as a form of antimodernism? Can we properly pick and choose which parts of science we accept and which we denigrate? Can we deny the mechanistic nature of science and reject some of its technological advances such as industrial farming, but then accept other parts that seem to suit our purposes? Is not climate science a part of the reductive and mechanistic mindset and do they not depend on the same technologies and assumptions as industrial applications?

Perhaps the Prince might argue in his own defence that climate scientists are taking what he terms a 'whole-istic' view and so see the proper connections between humans and Nature. This may be so, and indeed there are now many scientists who would adopt the Gaia concept of the earth as a unified whole. However, these climate scientists, regardless of their intentions, are still using the same assumptions and processes, the same means of calculation, to reach their conclusions as those who use technology and science to create drugs, fertilisers and genetically modified crops. Is it really acceptable to use science when we wish to predict the climate but to reject it when it comes to ensuring cheap food that can feed the world's population?

But the critique of the Prince's position might be taken further. He acknowledges that ancient societies were often brutal and unequal and those at the bottom of these societies often had short and unpleasant lives. These societies lacked much we now take for granted, such as healthcare, good nutrition and sound buildings. He admits that science has helped rid the world of many problems such as infectious diseases, high child mortality and ignorance. This might suggest that some, or even many, of the problems of modernity might also be its benefits: cheap food is possible because of industrial farming and cutting down rain forests; mobility and domestic comfort mean high energy usage, and so on.

So where does this leave the Prince's critique of modernity? Is it contradictory or incoherent for him to take his apparently ambivalent attitude to modern science? Are we really ever likely to be prepared to give up our comforts, let alone the liberties and freedoms of the democratic world? It is all very well saying humanity needs to return to harmony with nature, but what happens if this means we get cold and wet? Indeed how could this change be achieved? Who would impose it and why would we let them? It might be the result of some apocalypse, but why would we want to wish such suffering on our fellows? Moreover, can the remedies proposed by the Prince ever be more than limited examples, nothing more than exemplary cases and therefore exceptional and never likely to become the norm?

These questions get to the very heart of antimodernism and reaction: just what can and should we do? We might take the view that we reject all aspects of modernity, whether it is industrialised farming or modern medicine. Or we could simply withdraw to our studies – or public engagements – and ignore the world and all its contradictions.

This inaction, however, clearly does not appeal to the Prince. He seems to suggest that at this point in time there is simply no alternative but to act. The changes we have to take are absolutely necessary if the planet and humanity are to survive. The only alternative is catastrophe. This leads the Prince to propose a radical agenda for change, just as the same fear may lead certain so called 'hard' antimodernists to take direct action to convince others of their views.

But the problem with antimodernists like the Prince of Wales, for all the sincerity of his argument and the good sense of reminding us of the importance of tradition, is that were he to be listened to, and his plans acted upon, the result would be fundamental change. Furthermore, this change would be done on exactly the same premises as the progressive: on the promise of a better future. What the Prince is arguing for is a utopian vision of how our society might be were we to adopt the virtuous path he has laid out for us.

But why would the majority of us accept this? The sheer scale of the changes proposed by the Prince is simply beyond comprehension for most of us. It would be a 'year zero' approach akin to a return to the Stone Age where we would deliberately or be forced to forego all we have come to know and rely on. This form of antimodernism is too close to the radicalism it seeks to reject. It actually stops being reactionary and becomes a form of progress.

This points to the key problem for the reactionary: how can we be against the modern world, be critical of progress, and yet call for change? The Prince of Wales, as we have seen, argues for what he calls a 'sustainability revolution' (2010, p.3). We can see no attempt at irony here, even though he defines sustainability as that which endures. He is therefore calling for a revolution – a fundamental upheaval or rupture – to create a society where things endure, and where presumably there would be no need for revolutions. This shows the great difficulty for reaction: what methods can be employed to try to achieve our agenda? Can we use methods that are contradictory to our ideals? Many would argue that it is not possible to do this: it can only be achieved if we can compartmentalise our thoughts and ignore the intellectual contradictions. We might do this if we feel, like the Prince, that the issue is simply so very important. But others might also think that this so compromises the notion of antimodernism as to make the principles redundant: if all antimodernists can do is ape the progressives, what is their point?

So what can a reactionary actually do? Is it possible to get involved in society without also committing to change? Or do we have to accept the argument of Nicolas Gomez Davila we considered in chapter one, who suggests that the reactionary can do nothing more than sow doubt and suspicion? Is it always an error for a reactionary to suggest anything positive? Must the reactionary always have to live with contradiction? Perhaps this more than anything will tell us why a reactionary is often reluctant to claim the title.

But we need to appreciate that politics is often relative, or a matter of degree. It is seldom a case of all or nothing, unless, that is, we inhabit the extremes. So socialists do not necessarily reject all elements of a capitalist society. They do not withdraw from it even as they criticise it. They too have to make a living and eat and drink (whether they choose champagne or an honest mug of tea). They work within the prevailing culture, seeking to use the current institutions to move nearer to the type of society they crave. In doing so, they accept the right of those who oppose their views to use the same avenues to promote their causes. Likewise, conservatives have come to accept much of the modern socialist-inspired welfare state. So we might see reaction as a matter of degree and not as a pure or total condition. Indeed, to do otherwise would be to accept too much of modernism. Instead we operate within the confines of what is acceptable discourse within a particular culture. There are boundaries to what is allowable and we tend to operate readily within these, with only a very few who will seek to operate at the extremes, beyond civilised discourse. Indeed it is extremely difficulty to work outside of the established discourse and be heard. Michael Moore can only make his films and Naomi Klein is only able to publish her books within the capitalist system they condemn because there is a market for their work: their work is seen as profitable to those who run film production and publishing companies. If we simply were to assume that these people were just hypocrites then no form of political action would ever be possible. The only alternative would be cynical apathy and inertia. If compromise were not allowed, any form of civilised politics would become impossible. For some reactionaries this might have some appeal, but only if they can live within the current conditions without wanting any form of change. For those reactionaries and antimodernists who are not content, the only alternative then is to engage with the world as it is, and this may well mean using tactics that are neither of their own making or desiring.

I wish to suggest that it is entirely possible to be an antimodern without actively seeking the destruction of the modern. We can see our role as being one of critique, as sowing doubt and disillusion. We can reserve ourselves to showing up the faults of the modern world and so hope to mitigate some of these problems. But we do not seek to overthrow or destroy a civilisation. We choose not to do this because we can have no certainty over what would be left or come to pass as a result of our actions. If the problem is change and progress, then the thing we should seek to do is to prevent change and progress. If we have to live with the consequences of this lack of change then so be it.

Chapter Five

Prejudice

I

There is a common perception – the easy view, as it were – that reactionaries are not at ease with either themselves or the world around them. It is said that they are out of step with the majority. As a result they are prone to anger and the uncontrolled rant against those things that they disagree with. Reactionaries stand and shout, fulminating against the world and, like the unfortunate King Canute, try vainly to turn back the tide of progress. But, much to the amusement of all, they fail.

But, after all we have said, how accurate is this picture of reaction? Undoubtedly it is possible to find those who rant and rave, be it on blogs and websites (and some sites are completely barking) or on Facebook and other social media, (but why are they using such new-fangled modes of communication?), in the letters pages of certain newspapers as well as in journals such as *The Salisbury Review* and *The Quarterly Review*. After reading these articles one can be left with the sense that Western civilisation is right on the very edge of collapse, under the weight of dumbed-down education, Australian soap operas, Hollywood, mass immigration and the end of civilised manners. If one wishes to look for the swivel-eyed irate lunatic they are not too hard too find.

However, we should not forget that ranting and raving is not the sole preserve of reaction. There are many swivel-eyed Marxists prone to a bit of hysteria too. It is not hard to find a splenetic rant against Zionism, George Bush or 'Tory scum' on the web. A good rant and rave is not the sole preserve of any particular political caste. Indeed we should see it as a general disposition that some have. Of course, it is more likely to be at the extremes of politics, but it is by no means reserved to them.

Yet just as there can be civilised socialists, ranting and raving is by no means the only form of reaction. There is another form, which involves coming to terms with the world as it is. We know that there is much that is wrong with the world as it is. However, we also know that time can only flow the one way; that genies and flies do not go back into bottles; that we cannot unlearn things; and that clichés do not get any fresher the more they are used. Modern democratic politics is too established for a return to the pre-modern, and there were doubtless many who argued there was much wrong with the particular state of human development 400 years ago too. We know, through a reading of history, through the great works of philosophy and literature, and through absorbing and living in the culture that we find ourselves, what we have and what we might lose by chasing a utopia, even one based on the past. We cannot change very much and shouting louder will not make any difference: we have no choice but to accept where we are.

This form of reaction, then, does not seek to repudiate where we are and where we have come from. We recognise that there is much in the world to admire and that we would wish to retain. We can all come up with a list of these things, which will be eclectic and eccentric, ranging from T S Eliot and Ezra Pound, through to the novels of William Gibson; the films of Fritz Lang and Andrei Tarkovsky; the paintings of Peter Paul Rubens and Mark Rothko; the music of J S Bach, but also Olivier Messiaen, Dmitri Shostakovich and John Zorn; medieval cathedrals, the Victoria and Albert museum; Edinburgh, Delft, but also Cromer and Bradford. This, of course, is my personal list of fancies: it is my cultural baggage. Many items on this list have not changed for many years, and I doubt that they will. Many of them are not reactionary in any sense of the word: indeed it hardly seems an appropriate word to try to attach to them. And it is also not a closed list, but one that keeps growing and being added to, and occasionally things drop off as if by accident or due to neglect. There is, then, a lot to revel in within our world. We can take solace in much if we choose to.

In any case, our reaction is often only partial: we might be opposed to political change, but be rather different in our musical tastes. There is nothing unusual in this: I know several socialists who cannot listen to anything after Bach.

Perhaps it is safer to suggest that we are all reactionary in some senses: some are more reactionary than others, of course, but only ever in some senses. This means that we will be content about some areas of our lives, but disaffected in others. It might be that the disaffection overwhelms everything else on occasions, but it need not do so.

Reaction need not define us entirely. We can remain open to new things even as we eschew them in politics. Likewise, we can think of cultural reactionaries who are happy to countenance progress and reform. Reactionaries are no less open-minded than progressives: they are merely open to different things. It is easy to portray a reactionary as being closed-minded, but we need to remember that there are certain things that progressives will never countenance or give proper attention to. It is just that these things tend to be old, traditional and backward looking rather than new and original. There is a perverse belief that open-mindedness only applies to new and original ideas, and the progressive does not see it as a problem to dismiss old ideas in favour of the new even when the former are well-tried and are known to work. Progressives can be, and are, as closed-minded as anyone.

II

I suggested in chapter one that there are a number of basic propositions which unite the different forms of reaction and which might allow for some commonality across the very different forms in which reaction takes. In fact, I pointed to four such statements. First, there is a general sense of disaffection and disquiet with aspects of the modern world, which will be more or less manifest depending on particular circumstances. Second, many people feel that they are not being listened to and that their views are of no account. If they are heard then their views will tend to be discounted as bigoted or ignorant. Third, we feel that our traditions and our accepted ways of life are being threatened and changed without our direct consent and without seeking any agreement from us. Fourth, what we see as the 'establishment' — which, by definition, always excludes us — does not seem to have the same interests as we do.

It should be eminently clear that these propositions are not necessarily extreme, although undoubtedly they do not exclude the fundamentalist and the zealot. The propositions above might be used by an Islamic or Christian fundamentalist or by one of Julius Evola's secular supporters seeking to prevent Italy slipping towards communism (Sedgwick, 2004). But they do not need to be applied in this way, and just as there can be many different forms of socialism, which all begin with the same basis in equality and social justice, so we should not be surprised at the range of attitudes around these four propositions. Most of those who would subscribe to these propositions are not politically active and might not be sufficiently exercised to make their disaffection public. They would not see adhering to these views as in anyway extreme. They lead perfectly uneventful and moderate lives. Indeed, they would see the attitudes of the politically engaged, with their certainties and obsessions, as rather odd and extreme. For most people an active engagement in politics, whether it is campaigning, demonstrating or poring over blogs, is a rather bizarre and etiolated existence.

Part of the problem here is undoubtedly that those who seek to achieve progress, even in an extreme form, are perceived as more benign and respectable than perhaps they should be. In turn, reaction is all too frequently taken to be more extreme and with an ill intent. This is largely because those who write and comment on their activities are equally attracted to political activism. We can readily read in national newspapers and hear on the national broadcaster proponents of a so-called 'non-carbon future', where we would live largely without denuding the earth of its fossil fuels, as if this were somehow tenable and would not lead to mass starvation and authoritarian dictat. The idea that we can, and would wish to, survive without our modern amenities, even those as basic as electricity, or that we would countenance the huge social and economic upheaval of moving over to renewable sources of energy, is actually countenanced as a serious possibility. And what is more, it is, without irony, stated as a progressive notion, even though it would condemn much of the developing world to permanent poverty. One only has to list the commodities and activities that would have to be outlawed or heavily circumscribed — cars, planes, foreign travel, commuting to work – to realise just how ridiculous and otherworldly such a view is. Yet mainstream national newspapers accept it as serious commentary.

Perhaps one reason for this is that those who propose greater equality, social justice or protecting the environment can always portray themselves as moral and righteous. They are seeking to achieve ends that are essentially benign and good; they wish to save the earth or make us more equal. This can be contrasted with capitalists, conservatives and reactionaries who are apparently only interested in their own selfish ends, whether it is to make themselves even richer or to turn back the clock to a time when their interests dominated. Progressives, they tell us, are acting out of conscience and on behalf of others, while their opponents, who make no grand pronouncements on the future of humanity, are merely looking out for themselves.

It is, of course, one of the most benighted elements of politics to operate a differential morality: our opponents act in a venal or self-interested manner, or they seek to ensure society operates for some hidden interest, while we, of course, are selfless and pure in our motives. It is seen as scandalous and outrageous to suggest that we might be operating out of a particular interest even as we claim to see it quite clearly in others. We ignore the pointed criticisms of others, being too busy thinking up our own insults. All sides are as guilty as each other, of course. The problem, however, is the progressive does not have to work as hard as the reactionary to tar their opponents and exonerate themselves.

But how true are these four statements and is there any merit in them? Are we really not being listened to? Are our traditions under threat? Is the establishment different from us? And, of course, just how much disaffection is there? There is probably no way of actually finding out how far these statements are true. Or rather, more accurately, it would not matter particularly if they were found to be false. The reason for this is not because the questions are beyond empirical testing, but because what matters to people is the perception of these truths. They are believed and taken seriously by some, and empirical evidence to the contrary would not make a lot of difference. Indeed, any attempt to present an alternative view would tend to justify the initial perception. It would provide yet more 'proof' that we are excluded, not listened to and not taken seriously.

I do not believe this to be a particularly ignorant or stupid position to hold. Indeed it is little different from most ideological positions: not many environmentalists or socialists are dissuaded from their errors when presented with contrary evidence, choosing instead to attack the interests of their correspondent. If one challenges an environmentalist they will tend to assume you represent some vested interest, be it 'big oil' or agribusiness. We might suggest this is why Marxists invented false consciousness: it is a (perhaps unconscious) defence mechanism to prevent them from having to deal with the consequences of being empirically wrong. All of us perhaps think up ways to deny the possible falsification of our beliefs. So what matters, it being politics and not science, is the perception of a problem, and it is undoubtedly the case that these statements have some resonance. Many believe them to be true and act accordingly.

What is important to us are not the 'facts' – they can be endlessly disputed – but the baggage we carry around with us. A less troubled and more enlightened time would refer to this baggage as *prejudice*. This, of course, can be taken to mean literally to prejudge. It is where we come to a situation with a set of opinions and attitudes. We are living, feeling beings, with experiences and habits; we know something of the world, and we use this knowledge to help us understand the world. We judge a situation on the basis of what we already know. We do not come at something with a totally open mind, with objective reason and a forensic gaze. This has never been put more eloquently than by Edmund Burke, who extols the use of prejudice to distance the common sense of the English from the rationalism of the Enlightenment thinkers then so influential in revolutionary France. Burke explains to his French correspondent:

> You see, Sir, that in this enlightened age I am bold enough to confess, that we are generally men of untaught feelings; that instead of casting away all our old prejudices, we cherish them to a very considerable degree, and, to take more shame to ourselves, we cherish them because they are prejudices; and the longer they have lasted, and the more generally they have prevailed, the more we cherish them. We are afraid to put men to

> live and trade each on his own private stock of reason; because we suspect that this stock in each man is small, and that the individuals would do better to avail themselves of the general bank and capital of nations, and of ages. Many of our men of speculation, instead of exploding general prejudices, employ their sagacity to discover the latent wisdom which prevails in them. If they find what they seek, (and they seldom fail) they think it more wise to continue the prejudice, with the reason involved, than to cast away the cot of prejudice, and to leave nothing but the naked reason; because prejudice, with its reason, has a motive to give action to that reason, and an affection which will give it permanence. Prejudice is of ready application in the emergency; it previously engages the mind in a steady course of wisdom and virtue, and does not leave the man hesitating in the moment of decision sceptical, puzzled, and unresolved. Prejudice renders a man's virtue his habit; and not a series of unconnected acts. Through just prejudice, his duty becomes a part of his nature. (Burke, 1999b, p. 182).

What is so acute in Burke's observation here is his ability to describe us as we are and not as others would like us to be. We do not act out of 'naked reason', but come to an issue with much of our judgement preformed. But, for Burke, this is not a problem; instead he sees it as the very substance of our being. It is what gives some structure to our sense of self. We are not just creatures with reason, with our head full of abstract calculation, but we come with a history, and it is this overriding element that Burke forces us to acknowledge.

We come to a problem not with an open mind. This would imply an emptiness, a lack of preparedness – a 'blank slate'. Rather we come with perceptions and ideals with which we use to judge that problem. These perceptions, what Burke properly calls prejudices, develop from the accepted ways of acting and doing. Accordingly, our use of them reinforces these ways of acting and doing and brings the problem into our accepted sphere. We, as it were, domesticate it through the application of prejudice rather than allowing the problem an opportunity to question our established ways, which would be the case if we applied abstract reason. We judge a problem on our merits, rather than on its own.

III

One question we need to confront is just how practical is reaction? How realistic is it to espouse it? If politics is, as it seems to be, always about moving forward, and if we are in a cycle where politicians cannot avoid – if they wished to – the positive rhetoric of progress and change, then what use is reaction? How attractive is it as an idea to promote and espouse when we know that progress is inevitable?

Most reactionaries simply do not want things to change, and they will argue this on the grounds that change is often for the worse. But this is often, indeed hardly ever, practical politics, and accordingly many reactionaries will not engage in politics. They will perhaps look elsewhere, to high culture, to books, art, music or religion, and keep quiet in public.

We might actually see reaction as hopeless and fall into cynical despair and withdraw from politics and engagement with others. Might it not simply be better just to hide amongst our books, artefacts and music, our reveries of the past and just to ignore these preposterous debates about the future? There is an undoubted appeal in this, and we have seen that this is very tactic adopted by reactionaries such as Nicolas Gomez Davila. Of course, this might be a move made not out of despair, but from a realistic view of the prospects of turning back progress. From our eyrie, we can observe what is happening and comment on it, hoping to be listened to by some and so have some effect.

However, we have to appreciate that there are costs in not taking part. Our withdrawal from society means that those who seek radical change have a relatively free hand. There are now fewer people to stop them, and so they might actually become more radical. Indeed our silence might be taken as acquiescence or even support. As we have suggested already in chapter three, our non-participation does not weaken an elected government: it may have less votes, but it retains just as much power over our lives.

Withdrawal might also heighten the level of disaffection and turn it into a more deep-seated resentment. Our passivity guarantees our exclusion and makes it a certainty that what we feel ought still to be ours gets ever further away. This will be our fault, of course, but this might do nothing to assuage the resentment. It might indeed make us feel even more bitter about our situation.

But worse than this, our withdrawal will mean we will have to give up precisely what we purport to believe in and what we seek most fervently to protect. It is only by playing the game that we hope to achieve anything and preserve those things we consider important. Withdrawal, therefore, is where we appear to cast off our responsibility to preserve and allow the progressives a free hand to act as they see fit. We are giving our implied support by sitting on our hands and choosing not to resist.

In response to this we might argue that the current life we have is the only one we have and so why should we be using it campaigning for a better one? Would this not really be something of a waste of our time and energy, to spend most of our adult life trying to persuade, or force, others to live in a different manner from how they currently choose to? Indeed we might see that such action is worthy of contempt and ridicule? We might argue that it shows a rather sad and misguided approach, to forego our own life for the possibly futile prospect of ensuring something better for others, who might, if they are lucky, be able to enjoy it long after we are dead. And indeed, for those of us who live in the West, is life really so bad?

Of course, most radicals and activists do live in the real world and access its comforts as well as face up to its problems. It is actually very rare for a radical to live fully outside of mainstream society. Indeed it is a very hard and thoroughly disabling thing to achieve. So, again, why should we want to?

Perhaps we should see radicalism as a disposition just as we have with reaction. The problem, as Starobinski (2003) has shown, is that, after Kant, there is a tendency to see progress, and therefore the actions to achieve it, as rational, while reaction is based on the passions. This militates against the idea of progressive radicalism as a disposition. Action, it is argued, must be based on rational deliberation. It can even be seen as having a scientific basis as the Marxists have tried to argue. In contrast, reaction is portrayed as an urge, a knee jerk response beyond reason. Of course, we only have to observe radicals demonstrating, as they did in London in late 2010 when the police were attacked and property was damaged, to see how absurd this attempted distinction is: radical action is clearly based on passion and often without any sense of reason behind it.

This perhaps suggests that reaction is as practical as any other form of political action. There are always problems in acting. It will involve compromise, but then so will not acting. We, therefore, have to gauge what has the greatest consequence, reaction or withdrawal, action or passivity. This says little about the form that any reaction might take. It does, however, suggest that reaction is a less perverse form of political action than its opponents often might claim.

Reaction is never likely to become a dominant form of activity, even if it is a commonly held position. As we have suggested it has no form of organisation and is unlikely that any would develop other than some temporary form when there is a particular issue that galvanises a sufficient number of people (as in the Tea Party movement). Indeed, it is this lack of organisation that gives the impression of a small number of isolated and obscure individuals impotently rowing against the flow.

IV

Is there any prospect of reaction being rehabilitated? Can it ever be genuinely popular? Perhaps not, and this is simply because of the problem with the label itself. It simply sounds too negative to have a wide appeal. The term 'reaction' has too much of a history and has become too closely associated with a negative form of political action for many to want to adopt it as a label.

But labels might not be particularly important to those who have no thought-out and consistent approach to politics and social issues. Most people do not feel the need to put a consistent and coherent label to their actions. Indeed, even those interested in politics might not wish to apply a consistent label, and this may be because they actually hold a mix of views: they might be libertarian on issues such as immigration, but conservative on others like abortion or welfare reform. It is only zealots who seek consistency either for themselves, or, more likely, for their opponents. Most others do not see the need for such consistency, but take each issue as it comes. Lack of consistency is not a problem for most of us: we simply are not prepared to see ourselves as being contradictory or confused. We quite properly see that this is just how life is, where individuals have complex interests and appetites.

In any case, commonsense reaction is not something that is named as such: it is a term that I have invented to try to make some sense of certain reactions I have noticed and have come to see as relatively commonplace. So most people will not acknowledge that they are reactionary even if this is in effect what they are. Indeed, even those who are more avowedly antimodern in their attitudes might not welcome being named as reactionary.

There are alternative labels that we might use instead of reactionary. There are certainly similarities between intellectual reaction and traditional conservatism – so called paleoconservatism – particularly of the type found in the USA, which is much more openly intellectual than its British counterpart. But commonsense reaction lacks any real counterpart within conservatism (unless, that is J S Mill's description of the Conservative Party as the 'stupid party' is taken as a plaudit), or indeed any other political ideology or movement.

We might find that many would locate themselves more on the right than the left, and that they may be more socially conservative than the majority, in terms of their views on certain welfare benefits and immigration, for instance. But they may not take the same view with regard to political and economic issues, and they may not even be consistent on welfare issues, taking a more benign view towards the NHS and old age pensions than social housing.

This returns us again to the issue of consistency and definition. Just how far are reactionaries consistent, and how far should they be? Doubtless there are those who favour the traditional in all things, politics and the arts as well as a sense of dress. This might be natural for some, but not for others who will instead be reactionary in politics but not otherwise.

But then we can always debate who or what is reactionary. There are those who claim Burke was, such as Zeev Sternhell (2010), but others like Conor Cruise O'Brien (1997) regard him as more of a liberal and moderate. The same applies to de Maistre, where views range from Isaiah Berlin's description of him as the father of fascism and nationalism (Berlin, 1990), to Owen Bradley (1999) who sees clear links between de Maistre and aspect of postmodern thought in the late 20th century. Similarly Rousseau has been accused of being the founder of both Enlightenment and Counter-Enlightenment thought. And what about the former leaders of the USSR and the current leaders of China: can we see them as radicals or reactionaries, and when did they shift from one to the other (assuming they ever did)?

Indeed where does reaction end and something else begin? Once we start to suggest that some change is acceptable are we still a reactionary, and if some change is acceptable, then how much, and why just that particular amount? In any case, as we have already argued, is not deliberately moving backwards, were it possible, itself a form of change?

These are difficult questions that are perhaps impossible to answer with any certainty, and we might have to rely simply on self-definition, in which case, of course, the number of reactionaries would be rather small. This leaves us then with the possibility that there may be many people who *are* reactionary according to the discussions we have had in this book, but who will either not be aware of it or choose not to use the label.

So it would doubtless make for an easier life to give up on the label of reactionary and to settle for something a little less coloured, such as traditional conservative. After all we have seen that tradition is of considerable importance to our argument. But, it is precisely because conservatives have adopted the idea of progress that we should seek to rehabilitate the idea of reaction. They have ceased to be conservatives in the manner described by Oakeshott: they have a purpose where once there was a mere disposition.

As we have argued throughout this book, the problem is with modernity and with progress. We ought to be honest about this and so seek to own the term that has historically been most closely associated with the fight against modernity and progress. That the term has a history is, of course, crucial in accepting this point. In using the term we connect with Burke and de Maistre and the great Counter-Enlightenment thinkers. We connect with the great counter-revolutionary causes and so make it clear that what we are concerned with is the protection of a civilisation against those who, from within, seek to destroy it and replace it with abstract and untried ideas based on unrealisable assumptions. The word reaction has a history and that is why we need it.

Reaction is what the fight against progress is called. It is what we do when we try to prevent the world we know being changed by those who do not really know what they are doing.

V

There is one rather vexed issue that has been barely raised until this point, namely that of race and nationalism. It is not uncommon for some link to be made between reaction and certain attitudes towards race. This is, after all, perhaps what occurs to most people when they hear the word 'prejudice': it is against people of another race or colour.

There are indeed those who are avowedly nationalistic and who see immigration as deeply problematical and call for its abolition. Immigration can be seen as one of the most fundamental forms of change we can experience. It can be seen to dilute a particular culture and allow for strangeness to enter into it. This is something that some might seek to avoid or to repel. As I have suggested in chapter three, opposition to immigration is one of those dividing issues between progressives and reactionaries. It is one of the issues that cause some people to assume that their government is not listening to them or working for them. Immigration is considered to be unpopular, with consistent majorities against further inward migration, and with some even calling for the repatriation of past migrants. Yet, we have also seen that overly robust views on immigration and race, particularly of the 'Enoch was right' variety, can stop a political career dead in its tracks. There is a consensus on how race and immigration can be discussed by politicians and in the media that appears to be out of kilter with public opinion. It is precisely this type of disjuncture that creates the commonsense reaction that I have discussed in chapter three.

Certain reactionaries have undoubtedly been overtly racist in their views. We can point, for example, to Julius Evola and his support for Hitler's anti-Semitism (Sedgwick, 2004).

Göran Dahl (1999) points to what he calls 'radical conservatism' and suggests this can link the ideas of Evola to such diverse examples as Slobodan Milosevic's Serbian nationalism, Saddam Hussein's Iraqi Baathism, Muammar Qadaffi's Libyan dictatorship, as well as the actions and attitudes of the Oklahoma bomber. He suggests that this form of conservatism is nationalistic, statist, but also culturally relativist. There is an explicit link to race as Dahl sees radical conservatism as volkish in its orientation, seeking to place the interests of a particular people at the centre of politics, and he can point to the examples of Serbia with its nationalist wars and Hussein's suppression of the Kurds in Iraq.

Dahl provides a detailed justification for this notion of radical conservatism, seeing it as a new phenomenon to challenge liberalism and the dominance of the US in global affairs. However, we do not have the space here to look at his argument in great detail. It is interesting, however, that most of his examples of radical conservatives are, by their own definition, socialists. Dahl, in creating this concept of radical conservatism, is therefore not describing something that has developed out of traditional conservative concerns. It is also not opposed to change, but rather more concerned with national identity and the creation of a sense of unity to maintain an internal hegemony, with race playing a key part in this creation of identity.

It is a matter of debate whether we see characters such as Hussein, Milosevic and Qadaffi as reactionaries. As with anyone else we might link the term with, none of these referred to themselves as reactionaries. But, as we have seen, self-definition hardly ever arises in the case of reaction. More important, however, is their attitude towards modernity and whether we can see them as opposing progress. I would suggest that all of these leaders were overtly modernist and sought to attain progress, albeit of a rather eccentric and perhaps perverse kind. My view, without indulging in a detailed critique of radical conservatism, is that what Dahl is presenting is not reaction, but a further form of modernism. Indeed, we might question how appropriate his use of the term 'conservatism' actually is in this case.

But to return to the problem of reaction and race, it is indeed not difficult to create a link between certain aspects of reactionary thought and race. The issue, however, is whether there is a *necessary* connection between them. In the modern world, with its fast channels of communication and easy means of travel, migration is always likely to be an issue. Likewise, the imperial past of many European countries, something that some reactionaries might look back on with a degree of nostalgia, has created links between Europe and the developing world. As a result immigration to 'the mother country' has become common, and often because, as in the case of Britain, mother has encouraged it. These links cannot be wished away, and nor can we justify the rather one-sided view that it was acceptable to colonise parts of the world in the past, but now to attempt to completely disassociate ourselves from these peoples who follow our religion and speak our language. As Roger Scruton has argued, and as we pointed out in chapter two, Western civilisation can be characterised by its cosmopolitan nature. Its intellectual basis was formed by Athens, Rome and Jerusalem; its literature is taken from all parts and it has continued to assimilate ideas – and peoples – throughout its long history (Scruton, 2007). According to Scruton, Western civilisation has always been open to ideas and peoples. What differs, however, is the current refusal to see Western culture as a sufficient whole and to instead replace it with a series of cultures, all of which can have equal standing within a society and make a call on the allegiances of people who would have hitherto been expected to be part of a common whole. The problem, then, is not immigration as such, but the replacement of the melting pot by multiculturalism, and the denigration of the host culture that must, for many progressives, go along with it. To make all cultures equal, the indigenous culture must be denigrated and its significance downplayed. A part of this is the rejection of assimilation and the placing of diversity in its place. We should, the argument runs, celebrate difference and diversity and oppose notions of a common culture that all should assimilate into. This should apply even where the host culture is open and accepting of new ideas and peoples, and where migrants form only a small minority of the populace.

The issue for reactionaries, therefore, ought not to one of race or even migration, but rather of the primacy of a particular cultural tradition and its acceptance as a condition of citizenship. This does not deny the place of diversity, but rather asserts that there should be some attempt at assimilation of newcomers into the prevailing culture. In the case of countries such as the UK and the US, we are all mongrels, products of a history formed by migration and settlement. This can be sustained, however, only insofar as there is a common acceptance of a culture. Once this is denigrated and all cultures placed on the same level as this indigenous tradition the outcome will be disaffection on the part of the majority.

Cultures clearly change – there is nothing that can be done about this, or at least no one has yet found a way – and conservatives know this. We saw this when we considered Burke's discussion on change and correction in chapter one. We should only seek to correct and not to make new. But this does not mean that we can pre-empt change. Indeed, it would tend to imply that we cannot. We hold fast and wait until a correction becomes necessary. What this suggests is that we remain aware of what we are and where we have come from – I take this to be what Burke meant when he praised the virtues of prejudice – and then to use this as the template for our response to change.

The very opposite of the Burkean view was demonstrated by the Norwegian extremist, Anders Breivik, who murdered sixty-nine young people in July 2011 apparently as means of signalling the 'fight back' against multiculturalism. Breivik in many ways cut the archetypal figure of the reactionary with his demands for a return to a form of society that was pre-modern. However, we should more properly see Breivik, regardless of his mental state, as a symptom of modernism rather than reaction. He adopted precisely the tactics of extreme change that has characterised the modern utopian. It is a form of thought and action that is completely alien to the mode of thought we have sought to describe in this essay. A proper understanding of the nature of reaction would have precluded the extremism that Breivik turned to.

I would assert that there need be no necessary connection between reaction and race, or indeed with any form of overt nationalism. If there is no tradition of this, as is the case with the English, then the role of the reactionary will be to maintain that rather understated sense of Englishness that has developed and is seen now as central to the particular character of the place and its people. It is this very sense of understatement that has allowed for the ready assimilation of others. We need to distinguish between the natural sense we have towards home, to the known and the comfortable, which leads us readily to accept a common habitual way of life, from those who see others as inferior and alien. We are prepared to accept many people into our home, and to be solicitous hosts when they are there. But we accept others into our homes on our own terms and expect them to behave in a respectful and circumspect manner. This is precisely what the Western tradition described by Scruton has sought to do. It only becomes a problem when others are given the impression they can simply take over the house and ignore the hosts.

So we can suggest that the sort of reaction I have been describing here, particular the self-conscious and intellectual variety, has no connection with racist and nationalist feeling. Reaction is not an ideology or a specific set of principles. It is a disposition and this suggests that it can enclose a range of diverse views: people react to different things. It is therefore not possible or advisable to be prescriptive on what can or cannot be reaction. As we have seen, it seldom is organised and reactionaries will not necessarily come together for a common cause.

This, of course, will not stop those who see the word reactionary as a form of abuse from making a connection between it and racist and nationalist arguments. For them, it fits their definition of reaction. What we should avoid is to take this particular view as all that there is to reaction.

VI

The final point I wish to make is that there is some reason to welcome reaction. It may appear to be backward, or to be a refusal to see the world as it is. But this is only partly correct: it is indeed backwards, but this means simply that it refuses to see the world as others wish it to be. Reaction – the scepticism, criticism and resistance to change – is always necessary because the idea of progress remains so central to modern societies. As long as there is progress, there will be reaction.

We cannot perhaps see reactionaries as offering a particularly good role model for the young, but they might provide us with a more than adequate template for how to grow old properly. It is the only way in which we can deal with the very real disappointments and setbacks which we will have to face as we go through life.

Reaction will always be old-fashioned and go against the grain: that is what it is for. It can never be at the cutting edge, nor should it wish to be. It will always be on the outside, and this is because it can never compete with the supposed glamour of the new. Reaction will always be distrustful of change, of what is new and different, and will not see the need to follow the latest trends. As a result, it is reactionaries who will often appear to be different and distinct: this is because they refuse to follow fashion. Reaction can therefore be seen as a necessary corrective to the over-stimulated progressives, who continually call for change and who have no problem with flux and uncertainty.

There is, as we have suggested, not just one form of reaction. We can point to extremists and those who resort to violence and are called reactionaries. We can even suggest that some reactionaries will see other forms of reaction as the main problem, as is the case with the so-called 'liberal reaction' of Geert Wilders. But then we can also point to many examples of socialists who went to extremes and used the very worst forms of violence and terror to pursue their ends. No one is immune to extremism and the allied delusion that they are the only ones who can be right. But just as we should not assume that all socialists agree with the ideals and methods of Stalin, Mao and Pol Pot, nor should we accept that reaction must be extreme. What I have sought to do in this book is to develop a fuller understanding of reaction. This is one based on culture and not notions of race or nationality. It is sceptical of activism on the grounds that change is always unpredictable.

It is based on disaffection with elements of the modern world rather than an overriding desire to destroy it. But even here I have shown differences in how reaction manifests itself. It can be elitist or populist, reasoned or inchoate. Much of what I see as reaction is quiet, commonsensical and based on critique rather than action. There is often no organisation present, or even the urge to do anything other than complain.

This suggestion that reaction need not be extreme opens me up to two possible objections. The first is that I have described reaction too broadly, including arguments and ideas that do not properly belong. This needs to be taken seriously, especially in that, as I have stated frequently enough, not many if any individuals choose the label of reactionary for themselves. I hope that this criticism has already been dealt with by the arguments in this book. I have sought to show that if reaction involves the rejection of the modern and the support for traditional and accepted forms of life, then it is indeed quite broad. What I hope to have shown is that there is a widespread element within societies such as the UK and US that is sceptical of change and that resents the distance between themselves and the ruling elites. I see this as a form of reaction, and do so because it does not accept the notion of progress as an end itself, but rather wishes to remain in one place. It is most assuredly a description that does not fit the model of the splenetic red-faced ideologue. But that is precisely my point.

The other possible criticism flows out of this final point, but comes, as it were from the other side. My broad definition of reaction means that some on the right might consider my definition of reaction as being too liberal and inclusive. The fact that I have sought to include those who are not overtly political, and not stressed the notions of race and nationhood, might lead some to accuse me of accepting much of the progressivism I have ostensibly opposed.[13] There are those who use Burke to justify racist views, and others who see the likes of Scruton as dangerous liberals. One can only respond to these comments with argument and dialogue. But one also might wish to know that if reaction is as common as I suggest, why should it be narrow and exclusive?

If this appears contradictory, then so be it. I have already argued that one of the characteristics of some forms of

---

13 This has indeed happened. Some so-called 'National Conservatives' are incredulous that I do not see race and the apparent progressive conspiracy of 'forced immigration' as the main issues. As a result I have apparently 'exposed' myself as a progressive.

reaction is its lack of self-awareness and self-reflection. After all, when it comes to dealing with our prejudices, there is only so much we can do.

In any case, why should we impose ourselves on others? Why should we be so discourteous and inconsiderate to presume that we know better than them about how they wish to lead their lives? This, we should recall, is the very conceit of modernity, that experts knows best and that to impose their vision is for the good of all. We can engage with others and seek a dialogue, but this does not mean we can cajole or bully them into our view. There are only certain lines we can take and methods we can employ in order to pursue our aims.

But we should also remember that not all that currently exists is wrong or unpleasant. There is much that we can live with, and we know this because we are currently doing it. Our lives are not all bad, even as we might not feel that we are consulted and that we are quite where we would like to be. This might make us think twice before acting, in case we risk the good by forcing change to eradicate the bad. We do not wish to be fundamentalist about our antimodernism. We want to keep our freedoms and our culture intact. We wish to preserve the values of a civilisation and we must be careful how we do this. We will tend to lack the confidence of the progressive, and so we have to consider that we might be wrong. Accordingly, we should minimise what damage we might do. We are not seeking a return to primitivism, as advocated by hard antimodernists such as John Zerzan (2005, 2008). We are not fundamentalist about anything, and nor are we anarchists or freedom fighters. There is a distinct lack of stridency in our disaffection. We are only disaffected by certain things and not by others. We wish to preserve and protect certain things and we need to ensure that we do not become complicit in the destruction of anything worthy in the process.

Naturally, this opens us up to the charge that we are compromising ourselves, or of not being sufficiently serious; that we are not being antimodern, traditionalist and reactionary enough, and doubtless there will be those who will say as much. However, we live in the world that we do and we cannot wish that fact away. We must accept what we have, where we are, and that we have to live with those around us. All we can do is to persuade, argue and engage and failing that then withdraw with good grace. This, most certainly, is a rather limited set of aims, but it is the proper and civilised thing to do. It is the only way of keeping intact those things that are most important to us.

Bibliography

Baltanás, J. (2005): *Walking Through Le Corbusier: A Tour of His Masterworks,* London, Thames & Hudson.

Benoist, A de (1993): 'Tradition?', *Telos,* no. 94, accessed at http://www.freespeechproject.com/telos17.html on 11/1/2011

Benoist, L (2003): *The Esoteric Path: An Introduction to the Hermetic Tradition,* Hillsdale, NY, Sophia Perennis.

Benton, T and Craib, I (2001): *Philosophy of Social Science: The Philosophical Foundations of Social Thought,* Basingstoke, Palgrave

Berlin, I (1990): *The Crooked Timber of Humanity,* London, Fontana.

Berlin, I (1997): *Against the Current: Essays in the History of Ideas,* London, Pimlico.

Bradley, O (1999): *A Modern Maistre: The Social and political Thought of Joseph de Maistre,* Lincoln, University of Nebraska Press.

Burke, E (1992): *Further Reflections on the Revolution in France,* Indianapolis, Liberty Fund.

Burke, E (1999a): Select Works of Edmund Burke, Volume 1, Indianapolis, Liberty Fund.

Burke, E (1999b): *Select Works of Edmund Burke, Volume* 2, Indianapolis, Liberty Fund.

Burke, E (1999c): *Select Works of Edmund Burke, Volume* 3, Indianapolis, Liberty Fund.

Burke, E (1999d): *Select Works of Edmund Burke, Miscellaneous Writings*, Indianapolis, Liberty Fund.

Callahan, G. (2009): Michael Oakeshott on Rationalism in Politics, *The Freeman: Ideas on Liberty*, Jan-Feb 2009

Dahl, G (1999): *Radical Conservatism and the Future of Politics*, London, Sage.

Elster, J (1993): *Political Psychology*, Cambridge, Cambridge University Press.

Evola, J (2002): *Men Amongst the Ruins: Post-War Reflections of a Radical Traditionalist,* Rochester, Vermont, Inner Traditions.

Evola, J (2003): *Ride the Tiger: A Survival Manual for the Aristocrats of the Soul,* Rochester, Vermont, Inner Traditions.

Fallaci, O (2002): *The Rage and the Pride,* New York, Rizzoli.

Fallaci, O (2006): *The Force of Reason,* New York, Rizzoli.

Graham, G (2002): *Universities: The Recovery of an Idea,* Exeter, Imprint Academic.

Gray, J (1993): *Beyond Left and Right: Markets, Government and the Common Environment*, London, Routledge.

Green, E (2006): *Thatcher*, London, Hodder Arnold.

Guénon, R (2001a): *Introduction to the Study of the Hindu Doctrines*, Hillsdale, NY, Sophia Perennis.

Guénon, R (2001b): *East and West*, Hillsdale, NY, Sophia Perennis.

Guénon, R (2001c): *The Crisis of the Modern World*, Hillsdale, NY, Sophia Perennis.

Guénon, R (2001d): *Spiritual Authority and Temporal Power*, Hillsdale, NY, Sophia Perennis.

Guénon, R (20001e): *The Reign of Quantity and the Signs of the Times*, Hillsdale, NY, Sophia Perennis.

Guénon, R (2001f): *Symbols of Sacred Science*, Hillsdale, NY, Sophia Perennis.

Harvey, D (1989): *The Condition of Postmodernity*, Oxford, Blackwell.

Heilbrunn, J (2008): *The Knew They Were Right: The Rise of the Neocons*, NY, Doubleday.

Jameson, F (1992): *Postmodernism: or the Cultural Logic of Late Capitalism*, London, Verso.

Jencks, C (1989): *What is Postmodernism?*, 3rd edition, London, Academy Editions.

King, P (2005): *The Common Place: The Ordinary Experience of Housing*, Aldershot, Ashgate.

King, P (2011): *The New Politics: Liberal Conservatism of the Same Old Tories?*, Bristol, The Policy Press.

Kirk, R (1986): *The Conservative Mind: From Burke to Eliot*, 7th revised edition, Washington, Regnery Press.

Lebrun, R (1988): *Joseph de Maistre: An Intellectual Militant*, Kingston and Montreal, McGill-Queen's University Press.

Le Corbusier (1927): *Towards a New Architecture*, London, Butterworth.

Lyotard, J-F (1984): *The Postmodern Condition: A Report of Knowledge*, Manchester, Manchester University Press.

Maistre, J de (1850) *The Pope: Considered in His Relations with the Church, Temporal Sovereignties, Separated Churches and the Cause of Civilisation*, London, Dolman.

Maistre, J de (1974) *Considerations on France*, Kingston and Montreal, McGill-Queen's University Press.

Maistre, J de (1993) *St. Petersburg Dialogues: or Conversations on the Temporal Government of Providence*, Kingston and Montreal, McGill-Queen's University Press.

Maistre, J de (1996) *Against Rousseau*, Kingston and Montreal, McGill-Queen's University Press.

Maistre, J de (1998): *An Examination of the Philosophy of Bacon: Wherein Different Questions of Rational Philosophy are Treated*, Kingston and Montreal, McGill-Queen's University Press.

Nasr, S H (1997): *Man and Nature: The Spiritual Crisis of Modern Man*, Chicago, ABC International.

Oakeshott, M (1991): 'On being conservative', in *Rationalism in Politics and Other Essays*, new expanded edition, Inadianopolis, Liberty Fund, pp. 407-37.

Oakeshott, M (2004): 'An essay on the relations of philosophy, poetry and reality' in Luke O'Sullivan (ed.), *What is History? and Other Essays*, Exeter, Imprint Academic.

Oborne, P (2007): *The Triumph of the Political Class*, London, Simon & Schuster.

O'Brien, C C (1997): *Edmund Burke*, London, Sinclair-Stevenson.

O'Hara, J (2010): *A New American Tea Party: The Counterrevolution Against Bailouts, Handouts, Reckless Spending, and More Taxes*, New Jersey, Wiley.

O'Hear, A (1999): *After Progress: Finding the Old Way Forward*, London, Bloomsbury.

Popper, K (1989): *Conjectures and Refutations: The Growth of Scientific Knowledge*, London, Routledge.

Prince of Wales (2010): *Harmony: A New Way of Looking at Our World*, London, Blue Door.

Ratzinger, J and Pera, M (2006): *Without Roots: The West, Relativism, Christianity*, Islam, New York, Basic Books.

Robin, C (2011): *The Reactionary Mind: Conservatism from Edmund Burke to Sarah Palin*, New York, Oxford University Press.

Sampson, A (1962): *The Anatomy of Britain*, London, Hodder and Stoughton.

Scruton, R (1994): *The Classical Vernacular: Architectural Principles in an Age of Nihilism*, Manchester, Carcenet.

Scruton, R (2000): *England: An Elegy*, London, Chatto and Windus.

Scruton, R. (2001) *The Meaning of Conservatism*, third edition, Basingstoke, Palgrave.

Scruton, R (2006): *A Political Philosophy: Arguments for Conservatism*, London, Continuum.

Scruton, R (2007): *Culture Counts: Faith and Feeling in a World Besieged*, New York, Encounter Books.

Scruton, R (2009): *Beauty*, Oxford, Oxford University Press.

Scruton, R (2010): *The Uses of Pessimism: and the Danger of False Hope*, London, Atlantic Books.

Sedgwick, M (2004): *Against the Modern World: Traditionalism and the Secret Intellectual History of the Twentieth Century*, New York, Oxford University Press.

Starobinski, J (2003): *Action and Reaction: The Life and Adventures of a Couple*, New York, Zone Books,

Sternhell, Z (2010): *The Anti-Enlightenment Tradition*, New Haven, Yale University Press.

Versluis, A (2006): 'Antimodernism', *Telos*, no.132, pp. 96-130.

Voegelin, E (1987): *The New Science of Politics: An Introduction*, Chicago, University of Chicago Press.

Voegelin, E (1997): *History of Political Ideas, Volume 2: Middles Ages to Aquinas*, Columbia, University of Missouri Press.

Waterfield, R (2002): *René Guénon and the Future of the West: The Life and Writings of a 20th Century Metaphysician*, Hillsdale, NY, Sophia Perennis.

Waugh, A (2001): *Closing the Circle: The Best of the Way of the World*, Basingstoke, Macmillan.

Wood, G.S. (1969): *The Creation of the American Republic 1776-1787*, Chapel Hill, N.C.

Zerzan, J (2005): *Against Civilization: Readings and Reflections*,2nd edition, Port Townsend, WA, Feral House.

Zerzan, J (2008): *Twilight of the Machines*, Port Townsend, WA, Feral House.

Index

abstention, 65
acceptance, 25-8, 38, 75, 94, 105, 130-1, 147
accommodation, 27-8
antimodernism, 13, 28 95-131, 151;
definition of, 100-102
Arab Spring, 79, 91
Austen, J, 28
autonomy, 80-1

Bach, JS, 133
Baltanás, J,109
Belloc, H, 103
Benoist, L, 119-20
Berlin, I, 98-100, 142-3
Blair, T, 84
Bradley, O, 143
Breivik, A, 147
British Broadcasting Corporation (BBC), 84
British National Party, 68
Brown, G, 67, 87
Burke, E ,12, 13, 18-19, 24, 30, 37-9, 42, 44, 46-7, 52, 62-3, 97, 102, 116, 137-8, 142, 143, 147, 150
Bush, GW, 132

Cameron, D, 84
capitalism, 57-9
Carlyle, T, 57
change, 14-19, 38-40, 43-5
Chesterton, GK, 103
commonsense reaction, 25, 62-94
complacency, 10-11, 76, 92, 101, 105
conservatism, 8-12
Conservative party, 1, 142
Constant, B, 33, 48
Counter-Enlightenment ,7, 37, 47, 98-100, 107, 114, 116, 118, 120, 121, 143
counter-revolution, 34, 41, 91-2

Dahl, G, 123, 145
Daily Mail, 83-4
Davila, NG, 21, 26, 53, 130, 139
de Benoist, A, 100
de Maistre, J, 5-6, 7, 10, 12, 24, 29, 37, 40, 41-2, 46-9, 52, 56-7, 63, 91, 97, 99-100, 102, 103, 120, 142, 143
Delingpole, J, 84

Eliot, TS, 28, 51, 103, 104, 133
Elster, J ,78
Enlightenment, 5-6, 33, 37, 46-7, 98-100, 109-10, 143
Evola, J, 20, 24, 123-4, 135, 144

Fairness, 87-90
Fatalism, 24, 32, 52;
see also withdrawal
Field, F, 70
Fortuyn, P, 3, 106
Foucault, M, 106

French Revolution, 5, 18, 32-3, 37, 120

Gaia, 128
Garnett, A, 1
Gehry, F, 117
Gibson, W, 133
Glorious Revolution, 18-19
Graham, G ,102
Gray, J, 110-11
Guénon, R, 13, 29, 58, 106, 118-24

Hadid, Z, 117
Hamas, 97
Harvey, D, 1-9-10, 116, 117
Hayek, FA, 23
Heffer, S, 84
Herder, J, 47, 110
housing benefit, 89
Hugo, V, 31
Hussein, S 145

immigration, 26, 67-9, 144, 146-7
Irish emancipation, 44
Islam, 4, 57, 59-60

Jameson, F, 116
Jencks, C ,113-14, 116
Joseph, K, 31

Keynes, JM, 86
Kirk, R, 93
Klein, N ,131
Kollhaas, R, 117

Lang, F, 133
Lebrun, R, 56-7
Le Courbusier, 108-9, 112, 113
liberal reaction, 3-4
Libeskind, D, 117
Lyotard, JF, 111, 114-15

Mao, Z, 45, 112, 149
Messiaen, O, 133
Mill, JS, 142
Milosevic, S, 145
modernity, 7, 63-4, 96-7, 104-5, 107-12, 114, 122-3, 125, 143, 145, 151
Moore, M, 131
Moxon, S, 2
multiculturalism, 3, 26, 50, 146
Murray, A, 1
Murray, D, 84

Nasr, S Hossein, 106
nationality, 144-8
neoconservatism, 36
Newman, JH, 57

Oakeshott, M, 9-11, 23, 55, 101
Obama, B, 15, 40, 41, 43, 91
Oborne, P, 84
O'Brien, CC, 142
O'Hara, J, 40-1
O'Hear, A, 98-9, 107, 110

Palin, S, 38, 91
Pera, M, 50-1
perfectibility, 33, 97
Philips, M, 84
Pol Pot ,112, 149
Pope, The 1;
see also Ratzinger, J
Popper, K, 6-7
positivism, 112
postmodernity, 7, 113-17
Pound, E, 104, 133
Poundbury, 127
Powell, E, 67
prejudice, 78, 86, 132-52
Prince of Wales, 1, 13, 17, 58, 106, 125-30
progress, 2-3, 20, 21, 32-3, 35-6, 45, 53-5, 95, 121, 134, 140, 143, 149, 150

Qadaffi, M, 145
Quarterly Review, 1, 132

race, 144-8
radical conservatism, 145
Ramsden, J, 58
Ratzinger, J, 24, 50-1
Reagan, R, 15, 37
Renaissance, 120
repudiation, 7, 19, 50, 93
Rilke, RM, 104
Robin, C, 11
Rothko, M, 133
Rousseau, JJ, 143
Rubens, PP, 133

Salisbury, Lord, 39
Salisbury Review, 1, 132
Scruton, R, 24, 29, 40, 49-52, 55, 58, 63, 93, 97, 102, 146, 148, 150
Sedgwick, M, 118, 119, 121
Shostakovich, D, 133
slavery, 44
Stalin, J, 45, 112, 149
Starobinski, J, 31, 32-5, 42, 48, 140
Sternhell, Z, 47
suspicion, 21-2, 25, 53, 92, 107, 124, 130

Taleban, 97
Tarkovsky, A, 133
Tea Party movement, 13, 15, 25, 40-3, 64, 71, 78, 83, 87, 90, 91-2
Thatcher, M, 38, 40
tradition, 113, 117-24, 143

Unabomber, 104
unintended consequences, 6-7, 8

Versluis, A, 103-4, 124
Voegelin, E, 111

Waterfield, R, 122, 123
Waugh, A, 4
Wilde, O, 63
Wilders, G, 3, 106-7, 149
withdrawal, 11, 23-4, 26, 139-41; see also fatalism

Yeats, WB, 103, 104

Zerzan, J, 104, 151
Zionism, 132
Zorn, J, 133